Fine DECORATIVE BOXES

Designing & Making Original Works of Art

 S0-BNH-893

Ray Jones

Terry and Mauna Evans

ANDREW CRAWFORD

Sterling Publishing Co., Inc.
New York, NY

Andrew Crawford's Web site is
www.harlequinac.com

Library of Congress Cataloging-in-Publication Data

Crawford, Andrew.
  Fine decorative boxes : designing & making original works of art /
Andrew Crawford.
      p.   cm.
    Includes index.
    ISBN 0-8069-9862-8
      1.Woodwork 2. Wooden boxes   I. Title.
TT200.C794 1998
745.51—dc21   98-4281
                                                                        CIP

Book Design by Judy Morgan
Edited by R. Neumann

1 3 5 7 9 10 8 6 4 2

Published by Sterling Publishing Company, Inc.
387 Park Avenue South, New York, N.Y. 10016
© 1998 by Andrew Crawford
Distributed in Canada by Sterling Publishing
℅ Canadian Manda Group, One Atlantic Avenue, Suite 105
Toronto, Ontario, Canada M6K 3E7
Distributed in Great Britain and Europe by Cassell PLC
Wellington House, 125 Strand, London WC2R 0BB, England
Distributed in Australia by Capricorn Link (Australia) Pty Ltd.
P.O. Box 6651, Baulkham Hills, Business Centre, NSW 2153, Australia
Printed in Hong Kong
All rights reserved
Sterling ISBN 0-8069-9862-8

CONTENTS

Charles B. Cobb

Charles B. Cobb

Terry and Manna Evans

PREFACE

Boxes are like chairs or wrist watches, compact packages full of possibilities. The function each needs to perform is, broadly, always the same, but there are an infinite number of different ways of designing and producing them.

Curved-form jewelry box, 13" x 9" x 5½", by Andrew Crawford. The interior incorporates two trays in ebony. The exterior is veneered with a green and yellow harlequin design, with detailing in dyed veneers, boxwood, and mother-of-pearl. French polished.

A box will be a box and work more or less efficiently pretty much whatever a mess you make of it, but boxes are difficult to make really well. Just notice the way people look at a box—they will go really close up and "peer" and "inspect," whereas with a piece of furniture the tendency will usually be to stand back and admire. For this reason a great deal of effort needs to go into getting the detail and the finish as good as you can so that a box that you have worked hard on and are proud of will survive this cruel scrutiny!

Boxes are full of possibilities. The function each needs to perform is, broadly, always the same, but there are an infinite number of different ways of designing and producing them—thankfully, no one has yet built (or presumably ever will build) the definitive decorative wooden box. I hope that you will feel free to adapt, adjust, customize, simplify, complicate, improvise on or even largely ignore the ideas I have presented here. Some of the boxes are designed to hold things, some are designed to be just boxes. Not everything in life needs to be completely functional!

If you want to plan your own from scratch, you can approach it "inside-out" or "outside-in"—depending on whether you have a specific purpose in mind or not. If you are designing a box to contain a certain number of specific items, you must design it from the inside out—that is, all the dimensions ultimately derive from the exact size of whatever has to go in it. Accurately draw a representation of the contents in their intended orientation, and then take your time carefully drawing in the elements of the box, building them around these taking into consideration the thickness of the sides, lid and base, lining, and so on. An allowance for extra space is important, so that nothing is wedged in too tight. Even the thickness of veneers needs to be considered when dealing with small items. It can be helpful to construct a mock-up just to check that everything fits as it should—a little more time taken making sure the design is right at this stage will save you a great deal later on.

If, however, all you want is a box, then design it purely from the point of view of how you want it to look. There is really no other consideration—you are free to completely ignore any of the above restraints and let your imagination take over.

As with all true craftsmanship, the combining of these two approaches—careful planning and accurate construction to produce an item that performs its specific function perfectly on the one hand, and which appears to be freely expressed, on the other—is a goal for all to pursue.

The experience you bring to these projects may be an advantage, but it is my hope that you will find that the necessary techniques are presented in such a way as to make them accessible to woodworkers of almost any level. These techniques require time and care, but none is really difficult. What you really need are patience and an ability to work thoroughly and methodically. In this age of lightening fast computer technology the opportunity to work at the steady pace that this wonderful, ancient, adaptable, and abundant material requires should be welcomed. I occasionally forget to appreciate this, and I know how vast swaths of time can simply vanish due to trying to rush and generally not paying attention.

If you consider yourself to be towards the novice end of the scale then have a browse around the "Basic Tool Kit & Materials" section to get an idea of what you may or may not need (or be able to afford!). You do not need to have a lot of expensive gear (some helps) and neither do you need a lot of space (again, some helps). Many craftsmen and women produce fine results with astoundingly few sophisticated tools, others seem to use the lot and achieve nothing! A balance is what to go for initially—a few good-quality basic hand tools and maybe a small band saw to start with.

Whatever your starting point may be, as a novice with just a few tools or an experienced woodworker with many, I hope that you will find this book to be of some value.

Andrew Crawford

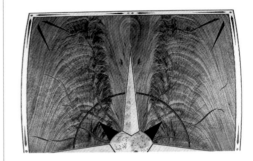

Large domed-top jewelry box, 21" x 13" x 11", by Andrew Crawford. The interior incorporates four trays and three drawers in bubinga. The exterior is veneered with walnut crotch with detailing in various natural and dyed veneers, mother-of-pearl, and abalone. French polished.

USING THIS BOOK

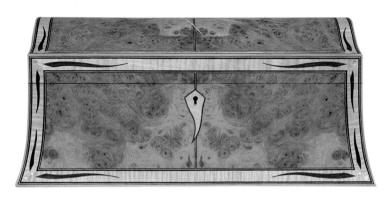

"William Blake" pencil box, 13" x 9" x 5½", by Andrew Crawford. Book-matched burr oak veneer with detailing in boxwood, mother-of-pearl, abalone, ripple maple, amd dyed veneers. French polished.

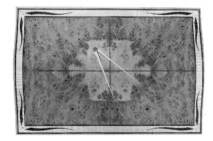

The interior incorporates five trays in cocobolo, lined with moiré.

In addition to the text and step-by-step photos, each project has its own set of plans and a cutting list—check these carefully and make sure that you have all the necessary tools and materials before you start. The sizes of the elements in the cutting lists are nearly all given in finished sizes. An asterisk (*) indicates where you should allow a little extra for trimming to length, etc., later. Most lids, bases, etc. need to be veneered before they are cut to size; so the sizes given for these are over-large to allow for this. The individual introductions to the projects contain any special notes that relate to the plans and cutting lists, so it is important to read these first. It is also helpful to read through a particular project text in full before you start it so that you have a clear idea of what you will be doing.

The plans are necessarily printed smaller than real size. You can photocopy and enlarge these if you like and this can be a helpful visual aid to see what exactly is going on, but I advise that you don't lift values straight from these enlargements. These plans were drawn from my original metric values (see notes on Metric Equivalents, on page 141) and they will not be exactly proportionally correct for the imperial values. In any case you may be adapting these designs to make them your own, and drawing out your own, full-sized plan is always a good idea.

Not all techniques required to complete a particular project will necessarily be included in the text of that project. Most smaller tasks are duplicated where necessary but some larger ones are not—a reference is always given so that you can quickly and easily find the relevant bit in another project.

BASIC TOOL KIT & MATERIALS

You will need some basic hand tools to do these projects—most of those described here will be found in most woodworker's tool kits.

There are often many ways of achieving any given task using a wide variety of tools. The tools I describe here are those I find particularly useful, but my list is in no way definitive. Don't immediately go out and buy one of every tool you think you might ever need. Rather take your time, buying the tools as you need them. Choose quality tools carefully and always buy the best that you can afford.

Using hand tools properly is difficult. To get really good results using hand tools alone, you have to be pretty good at it. Chisels and planes seem like simple tools, but to use them to their full potential (and maintain them) takes a great deal of knowledge and experience. A band saw (or table saw) and planer will substantially cut down the physical effort involved, but most operations can be achieved with hand sawing and planing. A router will further broaden your horizons and bring within your grasp the type of high-quality work you thought only professionals could produce. Once you own a few power tools, you will wonder how you ever got by without them! They allow even inexperienced woodworkers to obtain excellent results without the time-consuming process of being apprenticed to a master craftsman for 10 years to learn how to use hand tools properly.

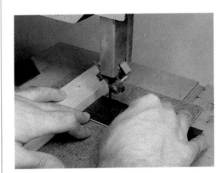

Power tools save a great deal of time and physical effort.

HAND TOOLS

This is my selection of essential hand tools. Most of these will be found in most woodworker's tool kits. You may not need them all right away, but all will be needed to construct the projects.

■ *Chisels* These are important and as with many other woodworking tools are available in a bewildering array of sizes, shapes, and prices. You should own the following: ¼", ½", and 1" "firmer" or "bevel-edged" chisels—firmer are the standard, square-edged chisels, and bevel-edged, as their name suggests, have beveled edges making them more useful for jointing, particularly for dovetails. It is best to own both forms but if you have only one, bevel-edged is best. In addition you should have a couple of narrower ones, say ¹⁄₁₆" and ⅛" for digging out for narrow inlays, lines, and so on. Finally it is helpful to have a few gouges—that is, chisels with curved blades. These can be very useful for removing waste from channels a small amount at a time where a straight chisel might not be appropriate.

One of my favorite tools is the cutting end of a straight ¼" chisel. It has no handle and no "tang" (the tapered prong of a chisel that fits up into the handle)—these broke off years ago, but I couldn't throw it away. Instead, I ground off what remained of the tang forming a smooth dome-shaped end; this fits comfortably into the palm of my hand—I use it for all manner of trimming, cutting and gouging operations. I use it particularly for removing the veneer from along the edges of a box where I am going to inlay a line and for cutting the miters in boxwood squares when they are already glued in place. The only problem is that I don't have a name for it!

■ *Clamps* A good selection of these is important. I have plenty of standard 3" C clamps, a few larger ones, a few sliding-head clamps with a longer reach, and some short framing clamps. If I need any longer framing clamps I borrow these from an antique restorer friend of mine—they're expensive!

■ *Hammers* Probably the least sophisticated and glamorous of all the tools you will use, but like many unglamorous things, it is necessary and invaluable. Two or three will probably serve all your general needs, but for box-making it is good to have an additional really nice, light "tacking" hammer.

■ *Handsaws* As I have a band saw I do relatively little handsawing. It is good, however, to have a good quality tenon saw for any jobs where band sawing is not appropriate, and a dovetail saw for dovetails. If you don't have a band saw or table saw, a couple of good larger saws are important—at least a rip saw for along the grain and a crosscut for across it.

■ *Knives* My personal favorite all-purpose craft knife is a good scalpel. I have gotten used to the feel of them—but use whatever you are most comfortable with. A scalpel makes a good knife—the blades are always of good quality, sharp, and relatively inexpensive. All of the general comments below, however, apply to whatever type of knife you prefer using.

I use a Swann Morton No. 4 handle with No. 25A blades—these are nearly flat but are slightly angled (second from bottom). This is a medium weight handle and I use it for a wide range of general cutting operations. I also have a No. 3 handle for very fine work (bottom) that I actually seldom use, as I prefer the No. 4, and a far chunkier "S" handle (top) for cutting up card and other more demanding purposes. The weight is very important and as with any tool is largely a matter of taste—as long as it feels good to use and does the job at hand efficiently. The thickness of the blade is important as using a thick blade to cut very delicate, dry veneers can cause the cut edges to crumble however careful you are. The finer the blade, the less this will tend to happen.

I use scalpels for all manner of cutting and trimming jobs, like cutting veneer to size and for the inlaying of fine details, but also for a few important scraping operations. When inlaying a line it is often helpful to very slightly undercut it—that is, make the cross section very slightly tapered or "boat" shaped. Scraping with a scalpel is a good way to do this: hold the line on its edge on a work surface and scrape the scalpel along, moving the hand flush with the bench to achieve a consistent angle. The slight angle of the 25A blade is just right for this. A curved blade—No. 24 or similar (second from top)—is ideal for many other fine, localized scraping jobs, either attached to a No. 4 handle or just used on its own.

An important technique when using any form of craft knife is to be able to cut around a template or a piece to be inlaid without cutting into the piece or wandering from the edge. This can cause the inlaid piece to be too loose giving a sloppy appearance to the finished piece. Be very accurate about the exact direction and angle of the cut, be sure that the blade exactly follows the outline. It is also important while making this sort of cut for inlaying that you use the knife at a slight angle so that you are cutting very slightly in, under the piece/template.

■ *Mallets* This is important for use with your chisels above—try to find a small carver's mallet (search a few old or "antique" tool shops) rather than the big, square, chunky type. Even if your chisels have the high-impact, shatter-proof handle, I can't really recommend that you use a hammer—I have no practical reason, it just feels so much better to use a wooden mallet!

■ *Planes* There are many different planes available for a variety of purposes, but the truth is that most functions can be accomplished with one plane. The one I use most is a Stanley No. 9½ A—if you have a planer/thicknesser, then this one plane may well serve all your needs. I have several other planes which I seldom use, but if you don't have a thicknesser you will need a couple of good quality hand planes and certainly one with a sole longer than 10" (and generally the longer the better) for converting timber accurately to the thicknesses that you require. With any plane check that the sides are square to the sole, and have a local shop grind them square if they aren't.

■ *Rules* A good quality steel rule is essential, preferably the anodized type for easy reading. I have a variety of these, but one 6" long and one 12" long will suffice for most purposes. In the project texts I regularly refer to rules as "straightedges"—which is not strictly correct. A true straightedge is not marked with any calibrations. For small scale work a rule makes a perfectly good straightedge.

■ *Scrapers* The best value tool you will ever buy—apart from a router—is a cabinet scraper. One attempt to better the performance of the simple scraper is simply to mount a scraper iron in a plane so that you can set a depth and use the sole of the plane as a fence.

Most useful is a rectangular scraper, but a curved scraper is great for shaping inside curves and for scraping down hard inlays. Sharpening a scraper correctly is important. A really sharp scraper should produce actual shavings similar to those produced by a finely set plane; but be careful, the blade can get very hot. Masking tape just above each of the four cutting edges offers some protection.

■ *Scribers* For accurately marking wood—anything with a good sharp point—the real ones often have one end bent around at 90 degrees, which can be handy in confined spaces. Particularly useful across the grain—along the grain it tends to follow it, not the straightedge—be careful not to use it too deeply as the marks can be difficult to remove.

■ *Screwdrivers* A couple of these should be in anyone's tool kit, but see remarks in "Cleaning Up Hardware," on pages 20 and 21.

■ *Squares* A decent square is essential; I regularly use a 4" and a 2" engineer's square. Good squares of this sort are expensive, but the traditional woodworker's wooden-handled ones are too big for this sort of work—and are just not accurate enough, particularly if they have ever been dropped.

■ *Thicknessing Gauge* This should really come under the "luxury" heading. The thicknessing gauge is a specialty tool used in the making of stringed instruments for measuring the thickness of sound boards and backs. It is a far more accurate way of measuring the thickness of boards than measuring across their edges with a steel rule and has the advantage that it can be done before the edges are cleaned up or the piece is cut to size.

POWER TOOLS

■ *Band Saw* If I had to choose between a band saw and a table saw, I wouldn't hesitate to say band saw every time—particularly if you do not intend to do a lot of heavy, large-scale work. It is far safer, in my opinion, more flexible, and user friendly.

Your band saw need not be large. Small, three-wheel band saws are the right tool for many light jobs. They have the advantage of having a smaller kerf, that is, they remove less material when they make a cut. This is particularly important when you are cutting strips of decorative line from a piece you have spent a lot of time constucting, as in Project 3, Jewelry Box.

There are a couple of precautions you can take to counteract some of the inadequacies of small band saws. Don't use the fence that came with your saw—it will almost certainly not be up to the job. It will probably be square to the front of the table, but that is often a problem, because the blade will not want to cut completely square. This is because the lightness of these small blades and the blade guides allow the blade to wander pretty much where it wants to go. Keep the blade guides adjusted against the blade as tightly as you can without actually stopping it from moving freely. The set on these blades can often be uneven, that is, the teeth are offset more one way than the other, causing the blade to veer in that direction. The trick is to discover exactly where the blade wants to go, and then to clamp a piece of wood across the table exactly parallel to that direction. A fresh, sharp blade and a slow feed speed (and minimum feed "pressure"—don't push too hard!) also help. For most jobs you are likely to do on a small band saw, one clamp to hold it in position at the front (near) end should be sufficient.

It can also help to have a piece of hardboard or similar material as a false table. Use the blade to cut the blade slot, pushing the piece on from the front, and then clamp the piece in place. You will then have a fine slot were the blade cuts, just the width of the kerf, and this can help to support the underneath of delicate pieces, preventing breakout.

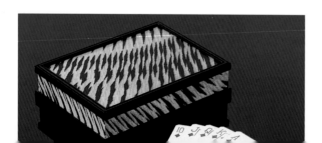

■ Electric Drill

Anyone who has done any work around the house probably owns an electric drill. It is worth owning a drill stand or "press"—this allows you to bring the drill vertically onto the workpiece with a spring loaded lever. A selection of good quality, standard high-speed drill bits is important, and in addition a set of "lip and spur" bits is good for cutting really clean holes.

■ Disc Sander This is the perfect tool for producing flawless miters with a 45-degree fence clamped to a table which itself must be accurately at 90 degrees to the disc. It allows you to remove the merest slivers of material where planing would be difficult until you have exactly the length you require. Both of these operations are very difficult to do accurately by any other means.

It is worth having a supply of parallel "packing pieces" so that you can change the area of the disc being used. This speeds up the removal of material and prevents scorching.

■ Drum Sander A dedicated drum sander is another "luxury" item unless you have a lot of that sort of work to do. All the smoothing of curves required for the projects given here can be done using curved sanding blocks and a little time and effort. I do use a sanding drum fitted to my drill in a drill stand. A proper oscillating machine is expensive but has the advantage that it oscillates to remove material quickly while not leaving any deep score marks.

■ Router The router is *the* modern woodworking tool. More than any other power tool it has brought high-quality woodwork within the reach of amateur woodworkers. I use a small router—an Elu 98E—mounted under an aluminium table, actually the table of my bandsaw. This arrangement offers a good space-saving feature for a small workshop—the only problem is if you need to do routing and sawing alternately, but this seldom happens. It is essential that your router is equipped with a fine screw adjuster for the height of the cut. It is simply not possible to adjust the height accurately enough for this sort of work without one. The router allows you to obtain excellent results without years of training.

I have a variety of mainly straight cutters, primarily from $\frac{1}{16}$" to $\frac{1}{4}$", but also up to $\frac{3}{4}$", and a few decorative curved and shaped ones. The small sizes are ideal for producing grooves to house all manner of ply and veneered ply pieces for bases, lids, and dividers. Be careful to choose cutters that have two flutes (cutting edges)—not one—and are "bottom cut," the type used for plunge routing. For grooves I use the cutter that is just smaller than the thickness I need to house, and then I gradually open up the cut using single pieces of masking tape attached to the fence until I achieve a snug push-fit. This is best done by cutting the basic, slightly under-size groove in a piece of scrap first, and adding pieces of masking tape to the fence until you have opened out the groove to just the right width. When satisfied that you have an accurate fit—not too loose but not too tight either—leave the tape in place and make the first cuts on the real pieces. Don't remove the tape and start again, because otherwise your second pass will be feeding an already thin piece of wood (the outer edge of a groove, for instance) onto the cutter in the wrong direction.

I regularly use the router in the projects to cut the lids off the boxes. I usually do this in three stages. I first cut a groove on the inside of the box pieces before they are assembled, and then, after the pieces are glued up, I cut a second groove exactly level with it to within $\frac{1}{32}$" of actually cutting through. The final breakthrough is achieved with a scalpel or similar precision craft knife. With smaller, thinner walled boxes, it is possible to cut only one groove using a fine, 1/16-3/16" cutter after the box is assembled. For thicker sides of 1/4" or more, such as a solid timber box or one that has been veneered prior to assembly, the width of the groove will often remove too much material to give a good grain match between the lid and the bottom. I like to match the grain all of the way around the box, but cutting a groove right through a 1/2" side in one operation requires at least a 7/16-1/2" cutter to get the required depth—anything finer wouldn't have the strength. If the box is being veneered after the lid is cut off, then this loss of material is not a problem.

■ *Planer/Thicknesser* This is an invaluable effort- and time-saving tool—the thicknesser part of this will quickly, accurately, and consistently convert endless quantities of timber to exactly the thickness you require—see the section below on "Converting Timber." The surface planer part has its uses but is often hard to use accurately.

USEFUL JIGS & AIDS

Several jigs are indispensable, for the router in particular, and many simple jigs and aids make procedures at the workbench that much easier. Nearly all of these, described below, are made from scraps of mdf (medium-density fiberboard) and birch ply, glued and/or screwed together. I regularly add to my collection of jigs as needed.

■ *Blind-Ended Sanding Board* This is simply a board faced with 180-grit garnet paper for 1/3 of its length underneath (see Project 4, Step 50). This is very useful for leveling the inside edges of trays, drawers and boxes—the unfaced portion of the board acts as a fence riding on the opposite side to that being worked, ensuring that you are working square. It is best used with a gentle grinding motion without using too much downward force—don't use with a backwards and forwards movement, you will just create a lot of unsightly grooves. The specific dimensions are not important, but it should be thick enough to be com-

pletely stable (preferably 1/2" or 3/4" mdf or birch ply) and wide enough to ensure that it remains completely flat during use. I have three or four different sizes for different box dimensions.

■ *End Stop* This is simply a piece of 1/4" mdf or similar material cut out to the shape shown in Project 9, Step 39. This allows for planing straight into the corner of a box lid or drawer, if you find that this is necessary. It also facilitates scraping at an angle across the grain of a prepared piece for a lid or base in order not to "roll" the grain as can sometimes happen.

■ *45° Block* This is made from a piece of oak or similar with a precise 45° slope cut at one end (see Project 4, Step 62). It is used for cutting miters at the ends of boxwood squares—the square fits under the block, and the cut is made with a sharp chisel while being held firmly against the front, angled face.

■ *No-Stop Bench Stop* This aid allows you to hold a small piece firmly for planing without using a bench stop. I use a piece of 3/8" to 1/2" ply or mdf about 12" x 4" with 180-grit garnet paper attached to both sides with double-sided (ds) tape. This is particularly useful when planing the edges of prepared decorative line planks, holding them in place with the free (nonplaning) hand.

■ *Obtuse Mitre Cutting Carriages* I made these carriages to cut the 67.5-degree obtuse miters needed for Project 10, Olly's Chinese Balls—see also the plan on page 113.

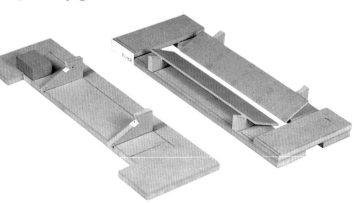

■ *Purfling Cutter* Purflings are the inlaid decorative edges right around the front and back of an acoustic guitar. A purfling cutter is the tool traditionally used to remove the material in order to fit these. I use one regularly in box-making for exactly the same purpose—it is the best tool for the job. Mine is homemade. There are many on the market but you will have to seek out a stringed musical instrument maker's supplier.

■ *Router Fence* I use a variety of pieces of wood and mdf fences that I use clamped across the table, but I have one piece made from 1" mdf that I use 90 percent of the time. It performs three very important functions: 1, for routing rabbets and decorative shapes along the edges of boards; 2, for routing grooves along boards; 3, both the above when a piece needs to be held vertically.

I also use this piece as a fence for my large band saw—the cutaway at each end allows the clamped piece to be kept vertical without requiring the use of hefty C clamps.

The sides and edges of any piece used in this way as a fence must be absolutely straight and square.

■ *Router Miter Key* A simple miter-key cutting carriage is invaluable for cutting the slots in the corners of trays and small boxes to take decorative miter strengthening keys. Ensure that it is set up truly vertically and that there is enough depth (front to back) to ensure that the carriage is stable on the table. These slots are difficult to cut in accurately by hand.

■ *Router "T" Bar Setup* A "T" bar is essential for keeping pieces that need to be at 90 degrees to the fence absolutely square and steady (see Project 4, Step 16).

The "T" bar is easily made and it is worth it's weight in gold. I use mine constantly. For some operations it is possible to use a simple piece of mdf with an accurate 90-degree corner to follow behind the piece being worked, but this is a less secure and the piece can twist slightly—support in front of and behind the piece you are working on, as achieved by the "T" bar, is preferable.

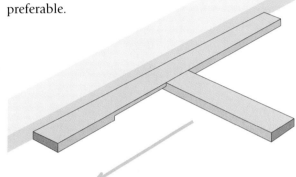

■ *Sanding Blocks* It is worth having several blocks and forms for sanding. You will need some flat and some with a few different curves if you do any curved work. Some should be cork-faced for general use, and some should be plain hardwood for leveling hard substances such as mother-of-pearl and SuperGlue. You will build up a collection of what you need as you go along. Always check for lumps on the bottom of the blocks before using them.

■ *Spring Blocks* As the name suggests, these are blocks that have strong springs attached. These are invaluable for holding small or awkward pieces against the router fence while each is being worked (see Project 9, Steps 8 and 9).

CONVERTING TIMBER

Before you start a project that uses solid timber, you will need to prepare the wood to the required dimensions. The following tips may be of use:

Quarter-sawn timber will, of course, be the most stable but is sometimes difficult to obtain in the dimensions you require. However good you are at hand-planing, you are unlikely to be able to produce boards as accurately and consistently as a thicknesser. If you own a thicknesser, a useful approach is to combine both methods. There are four distinct stages:

1. Band saw (or table saw) the timber to within a quarter inch of its final thickness. The more you think a timber might distort the more you will have to allow as you may need to remove a lot of material to arrive at your first, absolutely true face. Also, the more you stray from quarter-sawn the more you are likely to have to allow. Leave these rough-sawn pieces stacked up with pieces of scrap separating them so that air can circulate between them.

2. Plane one face absolutely level, square, and straight by hand—if you put a piece that has distorted slightly through a thicknesser, the rollers will just flatten the piece against its lower table during the cutting and it will spring back to its natural shape again afterwards.

3. Now run the pieces through the thicknesser, with the planed face downwards so that you are planing the unplaned face to within $\frac{1}{16}$ " of your required thickness.

4. Reverse again and thickness to the exact dimensions.

Always remember to allow a little extra length as all planers can dig in slightly at the beginning and/or the end of a cut. The amount will vary, but I allow 1½" at each end for a fairly small planer.

■ Awkward Grain

Some timbers will tend to tear slightly when put through a planer, particularly if the blades are a little less than fresh. It can be dealt with in the following way: Allow a fraction more thickness, and plane one face using the thicknesser. If it tears, turn the piece over and mark the unplaned face at the end that went through first. When you do the final cut, this end goes through first again. If it doesn't tear, turn the piece over, mark the back end of the unplaned face, and this end then goes through first for the second cut. If you only need one face, then this is all you need to do. If you need both faces, you will then need to reverse any torn pieces end for end and feed through once more to repair the torn face.

If it tears in both directions, you will have to resort to hand planing. Use a smoothing plane with a freshly sharpened iron, cutting at a steepish angle near to scraping, set to remove very thin shavings. If you have a plane with a sole that has an adjustable portion that can close up against the front of the iron, then adjust this as tight as you can while still allowing the plane to function, and this will help break off the chips before they can tear.

If you need to produce a substantial number of pieces with identical cross sections, it is best to choose a tangentially cut board. You can put the piece through the thicknesser first to define the height of the pieces, and then cut them slightly over thickness on the band saw.

Alternatively, you could use the router: First prepare all pieces by band-sawing and thicknessing to the exact thickness you require but slightly over-width, and hand-plane one edge of each piece square and straight. Set the inside of a straight cutter the exact distance from the fence that you require. As many pieces as you need can then be fed through this setup—from left to right so that you are pushing against the motion of the opposite side of the cutter from that which you would usually use to work the far edge of a board.

CHOICE OF VENEERS

The choice of veneers, and particularly the scale of figure they have, is important for the overall look of a finished piece. When buying veneer for small pieces you will often have the advantage of being able to choose leaves that other customers might reject, particularly with walnut, amboyna, or similar burr veneers. A good alternative to burr walnut is burr oak, sometimes called "Pollard oak." This has a lighter color with a fine, small-scale figure and some wonderfully subtle coloring.

■ *Veneering* I prefer veneering a prepared carcass made of good quality birch plywood rather than using a lot of solid timber. This means that a box can take a little longer to construct, but the basic construction is extremely stable. This is particularly important for the lids. Solid wood inevitably dries out and shrinks. Good quality plywood will not do this—it is really the best woodworking invention since veneers.

Burr timbers are weak and unstable in their "solid" state due to the wild directions of the grain, rendering them useless for normal construction. Basically, veneering allows us to use these beautiful, highly figured timbers to stunning effect.

There are now many ways to apply veneer, but it is the traditional image of pearl glue, messy boiling glue pots, veneer hammers, sheets of brown paper, irons and the like that has understandably frightened many away from what is a hugely satisfying area of woodwork. I know, because I am one of them. As a result I have never used pearl glue or a

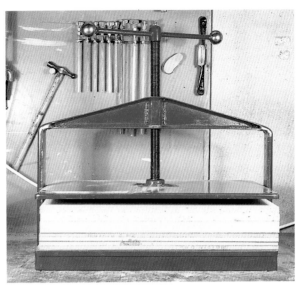

A Veneer Press

glue pot. I wanted to use veneers without all the mess, so I experimented, and I now veneer in what I consider to be a clean, easy, safe way.

This method involves simply using a paint brush to "paint" slightly diluted white glue (pva) onto the first piece of veneer—which is taped, good side down, onto a board. The piece to be veneered is placed onto it, and I paint glue on the top of the piece and then apply the second piece of veneer. This is followed, quickly, by a piece of paper, a piece of carpet underlay, and finally a second rigid board. I then put the whole lot in the veneer press, and in about an hour it is cooked. The carpet underlay is all important—it ensures a really even spread of pressure. You will need two good, solid, rigid boards—1" ply or mdf is fine—each about 14" x 10" (or to fit your press) and faced with formica or some other, kitchen-type work surface.

When veneering a board, you must always veneer both sides, preferably at the same time, to "balance" the board and avoid any bowing. Ideally you need a veneer press. You can veneer using this method without a press but you need to be well set up with lengths of tough angle iron—5 or 6 lengths to run the width of your boards to spread the pressure as evenly as possible—and plenty of C clamps, two per length of angle iron.

I dilute the pva with 10 percent water and this aids the process in several ways. The thinner mixture allows it to be painted—I usually use a standard 2" paint brush, kept in a pot of water. The higher water content allows the glue to "grab" slightly into the veneer in the same way as traditional hot glue. If it is left full strength, there is very little absorption into the veneer and the glue tends to sit there forming a barrier rather than bonding the veneer to its panel. Finally, the increased water content slows the drying time, allowing a bit of extra setting-up time.

It has its disadvantages—as with hot glue the amount of glue you apply is important, but difficult to quantify. Too little and you may find small areas where the veneer is lifting, too much and the glue can soak through, causing a patchy appearance when the finish is applied. Experiment!

FRENCH POLISH
& OTHER FINISHES

French polish is the undisputed king of finishes and really the only finish for high-quality cabinet work. It has to be said, however, that it is not that hard-wearing—but then boxes don't generally need to be hard-wearing. It is worth saying a word about the polishing environment and other finishes, but I will elaborate only on French polishing.

■ *Workshop Conditions* Polishing needs an environment that is reasonably warm and dry. This seldom presents a problem with modern central heating, but this in itself can cause an over-dry atmosphere which, although beneficial to the polishing process, is not so good for woodwork in general.

You will never arrive at a completely dust-free environment and it is, in fact, not necessary as the way polishing works deals with dust landing on the surface being worked. I do, however, try to minimize airborne dust during polishing operations. The evening before I want to do any polishing, I do the sanding operations necessary for any pieces in progress, dust them off thoroughly, and then place them on a high shelf (a separate room is better). I then have a thorough (but gentle) sweep up in the workshop and go home. I enter the workshop quietly and carefully the next morning, so as not to raise too much dust, and gently proceed to do whatever polishing I need to. I then replace the pieces on their shelf out of harm's way and proceed to saw, sand, and generally create dust to my hearts content for the rest of the day!

■ *The Rubbing Pad* The "rubber" (that which rubs, not the substance) is formed from a piece of lint-free cotton wadding with a piece of cotton sheet (rag) wrapped around it. The wadding is then charged with a small amount of polish, and the rag is wrapped around it and pressed onto a sheet of paper to distribute the polish and start it flowing through the weave. This unlikely bundle is the magical, miracle-working tool that countless craftsmen and women have used for centuries to apply this matchless finish to fine woodwork of all types.

The rag should be well washed and with as fine a weave as you can find—an old, clean, worn, plain white cotton sheet is ideal, but be careful that it is not rotten—this can cause it to wear through after only a small amount of use and shed its own fine, white dust which doesn't help! The size of the rubber is important—I usually use one with a working surface of around 1" x ¾", made from a piece of rag about 3" x 4". If you are not polishing a whole tabletop, a rubber the size of the palm of your hand is just not appropriate— I might increase the size a little if I am doing a really large box. Keep your rubber in a small, airtight container—a plastic 35mm film container is ideal for the small ones that I use—and add a couple of drops of meths to the face to prevent it from drying out between operations. Together with polish, white oil, and spirit, this forms the polisher's tool kit.

Traditionally, a furniture maker finishing a tabletop may use two or three distinct dilutions of polish during the finishing process and finally "spirit off" using a separate rubber. I tend to use the same rubber to finish off as for the early stages, gradually changing the proportions by adding more or less polish/spirit. The wadding used as the basis for the rubber can last for ages, and will gradually shape itself to the way you hold it and the way you polish. The rag, however, needs to be changed reasonably frequently, whenever the edges around the actual polishing surface become too black and clogged with dirt. This can scratch your hard earned finish and can be heart-breaking. I always use a fresh piece of rag for what I hope will be my final burnish, thus reducing this risk to a minimum. I apply the polish to the face of the wadding with the rag removed, a few drops at a time, and I don't usually open the wadding and feed it from behind as is traditional.

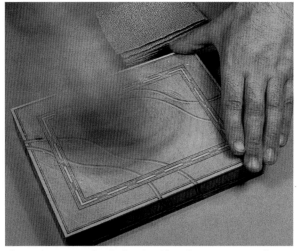

Arriving at a perfectly level surface by using a gentle grinding motion

■ *Achieving a Satin or Matte Finish* If I want a satin or matte type of finish I frequently use sanding sealer that is sometimes mixed with some transparent French polish, as a basic sealer coat, which I then cut back with 1200-grit wet and dry paper and wax. I seldom use anything but clear wax—I use a lot of light-colored timbers and bright colored veneers, and this allows the true colors to come out and does not force dark wax into the grain.

■ *Polishing Solid Timber* For solid timber I will often use teak oil or Danish oil. If I need a really hard wearing, completely filled, level surface I do occasionally use a modern two-part lacquer—many coats, each brushed on and sanded level before the next application—marquetarians will be well used to this. Avoid sprayed-on finishes unless you don't mind your work looking as though it is encased in a thick, gooey, transparent plastic shell.

■ *Filling Grain* Hard, dense woods like maple do not need much filling, but other, more decorative ones, particularly walnut (which is also very absorbent), can need lots. It is better to avoid using actual grain fillers as these can cause all sorts of problems later on. Color changes are common—even matching the color initially can be hard enough.

Certain small knot holes can be filled using solid shellac sticks, available in a wide range of colors. The shellac is melted into the hole using the warmed point of a small screwdriver—but you must be careful to match the color very carefully. The shellac will sink when you apply any finish on top, however, as it will be softened by the solvent.

It can be a long process filling the grain with polish alone. A mix of 50 percent polish and 50 percent shellac sanding sealer (SSS) works well; when applied with a brush, it will be harder than the SSS on its own, and more sandable than the polish on its own. It will also fill open grain well. Three or four applications, sanded in between each, should be sufficient depending on how absorbent your veneer is. A gentle grinding motion using 240- or 320-grit self-lubricating paper on a small cork-faced block is good at this stage.

■ *Using Abrasives* The type and grade of abrasive used at different stages is very important. During the early, building-up stages, 240-grit self-lubricating paper is best—French polish clogs normal sandpaper very quickly. Progress to finer grades in the later stages as the balance changes from filling to cutting back. I always divide my abrasive sheets into 8 or 16 handy-sized pieces for using with the small, cork-faced sanding block, or just with finger pressure.

■ *French Polishing* By French-polishing you can finely control the amount of finish you are applying, and, done properly, the final effect is that there is no visible "thickness" of finish at all. Another important way in which French polish differs from most modern finishes is that it remains "alive"—this allows it to be "repaired" far more easily, and also allows you to keep on going with the final stages until you have exactly the finish you want.

French polishing on its own is a huge subject—and some of you will already be experienced polishers. I will try to impart a general understanding of what is going on in the polishing process, but everyone will form their own ways of working and experience is really the only way to arrive at a method that suits you.

Broadly speaking, there are really only two things that happen in French polishing: building up and cutting back. The early stages are devoted to applying polish, grain-filling, and building up a good body of polish, and later on you will be cutting back and burnishing the polish that you have applied. The process of French polishing varies enormously depending on what timber you are polishing. Good

Adding layer upon layer of polish

woods are: cherry, yew, walnut, mahogany, maple, and any fine-grained and generally dense timbers—more absorbent, open-grained timbers will need a great deal more polish and time. It is not really appropriate to French-polish the most open and coarse, open-grained timbers such as oak or ash. The exception to this seems to be rosewood—certain species can to be very open and coarse-grained, requiring a considerable amount of work to build up a level, filled surface. This work is well rewarded, however, by the wonderful colors that the polishing process brings out.

Be aware that the lighter your polish (I use transparent for almost everything) the shorter its shelf life. I buy transparent polish in the smallest quantities available and only keep it about four months before I ditch it and buy a new lot. If you persevere with polish that is older than about six months you will find that it will not harden properly, and it will be very difficult to achieve a really stable, clear finish. It will also be very prone to picking up dust particles during the early, building up stages.

■ *Building up Polish* Once a level surface has been achieved, the building up of polish is done by going over the surface with the charged rubber, again and again, adding layer upon layer of polish—don't use any spirit at this stage, but after your first few passes use a small amount of white oil applied to the face of the rubber to allow it to move freely. Always start the rubber in motion before it is in contact with the surface and sweep it off the other end. Ensure that you work right up to all edges and corners. Each layer will be microscopically thin and will appear to dry almost instantly. A light positioned so that it is reflected exactly where you are working will reveal a sort of "vapour trail" behind the moving rubber as the majority of the spirit evaporates within a fraction of a second. A finger brushed along the surface immediately will not encounter any wetness—the feel will be smooth with no hint even of stickiness, so long as the finger keeps moving. The polish will, however be very soft and vulnerable, which is why the rubber must never stop while doing its work—otherwise it will stick and leave an imprint of its weave on your evolving surface.

As the polish gradually builds up and this drying becomes less instantaneous, the rubber will start to drag. This is good as the friction will be leveling the surface as well as building it up. If you start to feel a rough, scraping sensation, however, this is not good and you need a little more oil. Apply this a drop at a time to the face of the rubber after you have charged it, adding just enough to keep the rubber moving with a bit of healthy friction but not so much that the rubber slithers on the surface. This is an essential part of the polishing process—use it reasonably liberally in the early stages to allow plenty of polish to build up without the rubber sticking to the increasingly soft polish underneath.

There is a limit, however, to how much polish you can apply to one surface in one sitting. As I have said, French polish dries to the touch almost instantly, but if you continue working on one area for too long, it will start to retain a certain stickiness and any dust that lands on your surface will tend to stick to it, rather than just sitting there waiting to be swept off by the rubber on its next pass. This sweeping up of various particles of dirt and dust is an essential part of the polishing process and is, in part, the cause of the dark crust that forms around the rag of your rubber, necessitating its eventual replacement.

If you notice any specks of dirt sticking to the surface, stop working on that area and move on to another.

Allowing time for the polish to settle is important. You will think that you have arrived at a completely filled surface only to find, a day or two later, that it has sunk again. This is because the spirit that is the solvent continues to evaporate.

■ *Getting That Bright, Clear Finish* The progression you should bear in mind throughout the polishing process is from initially using neat polish to build up right through to using neat spirit at the end to give the final, bright, clear finish that is the hallmark of a well-polished piece. Having arrived at a good, level body of polish, the actual addition of further polish should be reduced and the balance should gradually change from filling and building up to cutting back and burnishing.

Pay close attention around the edges.

Sand with 240-, 320-, and then 400-grit self-lubricating paper progressing to finer grades as the balance gradually changes from filling to cutting back. Then in the later stages use only 1200-grit wet & dry paper to arrive at a perfectly level, creamy matte surface. Pay close attention around the edges (particularly if you have inlaid decorative bandings—these will be more absorbent than the surrounding veneer and more prone to tiny dips). Maintain a consistent direction when sanding the finish at this stage. This is an operation that takes time but is well worth it—the wet and dry paper will clog quickly and will have to be discarded almost as soon as you have started to use it.

At this stage there should be no detectable low spots, that is, areas that still reflect light. These should have all been sorted out earlier. If you do find any that you have missed—or have ignored at an earlier stage hoping that they will go away—these can be filled using the gel-like version of SuperGlue or a similar clear adhesive. Apply a small amount using the point of a scriber, allow it to dry, and sand flush using 400-grit self-lubricating paper around a small, hardwood block. This needs to be done very carefully. Don't use a cork-faced block. The glue is much harder than the polish, and it is easy to cut this back rather than the glue. When completely flush, sand with 1200-grit wet & dry again, using only very gentle finger pressure.

The task now is one of removing (partly by a small amount of filling, but mainly by cutting back and burnishing) the marks left by the last sanding operation. It is good to keep the rubber "drier" during these crucial later stages. Work steadily and confidently, starting with smooth passes along the length of the area you are working on, polishing with the grain. Then work across it, then in wide, elliptical motions, and proceed to circular, gradually increasing the pressure all the time as the function of the rubbing changes from filling to cutting as it dries out.

■ *The Final Stages* I use only the very smallest amount of polish and a little more spirit in the final stages. Press the rubber on paper to start the flow, and start with gentle, swift strokes along and then across the grain. This will soften the polish very slightly and dry out the rubber for the true burnishing. This is done with firm, small, circular movements using much more pressure than when you were applying polish.

A Suggested Schedule

I tend to work according to the following schedule: I do the early, building up stages with the box in separate pieces—box and lid. I spend a few minutes working on each individual surface, recharging the rubber perhaps six or eight times, and then proceed to the next, and so on, until I have done each surface. I will then repeat this immediately and continue throughout the surfaces until I have worked on each surface five or six times. I then set the pieces aside until that evening, sand all surfaces, sweep up, and go home. I repeat the process the next day, and for the next three or four days until I have a good body of polish built up, and leave it to rest for another three or four days. I then start using the spirit and a bit less polish and similarly rotate through the surfaces, but with more setting aside time, say two days, and repeat this three or four times. When I am nearing the end of the polishing process, I give the back of both lid and box a final burnish, first with only a little polish, and then with just spirit, to as good a finish as I can.

This is the final go at the back since it is hard to work on with the hinges fitted—I then refit the hinges using brand new, polished screws(see "Cleaning Up Hardware").

Finally I do the last polishing and burnishing operations with the box in one piece, working over each side and the front as single areas. For these final stages I will again set the box aside for three or four days at a time. Take special care when you come to do the lid—this is what will reflect the light, showing any flaws!

Final polishing and burnishing with the box all in one piece

CLEANING UP HARDWARE

Suitable hardware is difficult to find. It is worth being able to make the best of what's available.

■ *Cheap Catches & Nasty Lacquer* Small catches, hinges, and other fittings intended for cheap "trinket" type boxes are often of poor quality, brass-plated rather than solid brass, and coated with really nasty, shiny lacquer. These are sometimes appropriate because of their small size. You will want to remove the lacquer. Use 0000 wire wool—this should give a more friendly finish that looks far more like real brass. Many of these fittings are intended to be fastened using fine pins, which generally will not hold them in place securely. Drill out any holes for these pins and countersink to fit fine brass machine screws. These little machine screws are threaded for the whole of their length, making them ideal for fastening hardware to very thin-walled boxes. The size of drill to make the hole in the wood to take these screws should be about the diameter of the core of the screw. Use a screwdriver that fits the slots of your screws like a glove, is the full width of the slot, and preferably fits so well that you can push the screw onto the end so that it stays. It is also worth slightly rounding over the bottom corners of the blade so they don't cut into the material.

■ **Final Construction** Don't do these various cleaning up operations until you have fitted the locks, lined up hinges, etc., and are ready to put your work together for the last time. Only use your polished screws for this final putting together—and remember to line up the slots!

■ **Hinges** The knuckles are often uneven and unmatched. With the hinge closed, hold the knuckle against the side of a medium-grit grinding wheel. Be careful: it will get very hot—dunk it in water or hold it with a piece of cardboard. Gently rotate the hinge about its pin to remove any coarse marks left in its manufacture, to produce an even, matched surface.

Now work on the hinge with 400-, then 600-, 800- and finally 1200-grit wet and dry paper, used wet, working in the direction of the knuckle and rotating as when grinding to obtain an even finish.

■ **Locks** The locks themselves are generally easy to clean up, especially if they are being used where the interior is lined, thus covering up the inside plate. Use the same progression of abrasives as for the hinges, but go easy on the water to avoid rusting, finishing with 0000 wire wool.

If the whole lock is to be exposed, you will need to clean up the back of the lock a little—but don't be tempted to grind this plate flat as you may well destroy the small rivets that hold the lock together.

Work the top plates with a "safe-edge" needle file, so that you can file right up to the edge of the "prongs" without damaging them. Work through the grades as before.

■ **Matching Screws** Having cleaned up the rest of your hardware, the screw heads should match! It is worth making up a block to facilitate this job. I

Refitting the hinges with new, polished screws

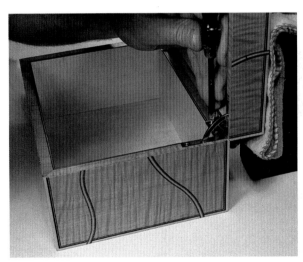

Final construction—putting the work together for the last time

suggest that a third of the block be for screws with the rest of the length being to hold the sanding block level. Some 180-grit garnet paper fixed to the base will stop it moving around while you are working. Drill holes so that the screws screw in easily. Countersink so that only about $\frac{1}{64}$" or less of the head is proud. Now use a sanding block faced with cork, some 1200-grit wet and dry paper, and a little water. Work gently over the screws using a circular, grinding motion. Proceed to polishing paper and jeweler's rouge if you like.

1 DISKETTE BOX

This colorful box is designed to hold around 50 3½" floppy computer disks. Its interior dividers are removable so that when floppies eventually become extinct (which they surely will) the box can be used for something else.

The pieces for the front, back, and sides are made from ⅜" birch ply with a single piece of maple lipping along the bottom of each piece to take the base. The box is tongue jointed, the main advantage being that if the plywood "biscuits" fit snugly, you only need to clamp up in one direction (front to back) because they register the end-to-end dimension perfectly securely. The entire exterior and interior of the box are veneered, including its inner edges.

■ *Wavy Lines* These are formed from laminating dyed veneers in an mdf form with a freehand wavy line cut through it on the band saw. Slices are then cut from the edge of this prepared sandwich to give you your individual lines ready for inlaying. I have chosen two different lines for this project, a rainbow version and a blue/green version, each using eight strips per line. You can use more but the thicker the lines get the more the final, clamped-up piece will suffer from a variation in thickness due to the curves. This sort of set-up will take a while to dry properly—the increased water content in the diluted PVA and the fact that you have a relatively high quantity of glue in a small, confined space will both have the effect of increasing the drying time. If allowed to dry properly (about two hours should do it) the individual lines cut from this sandwich are surprisingly strong.

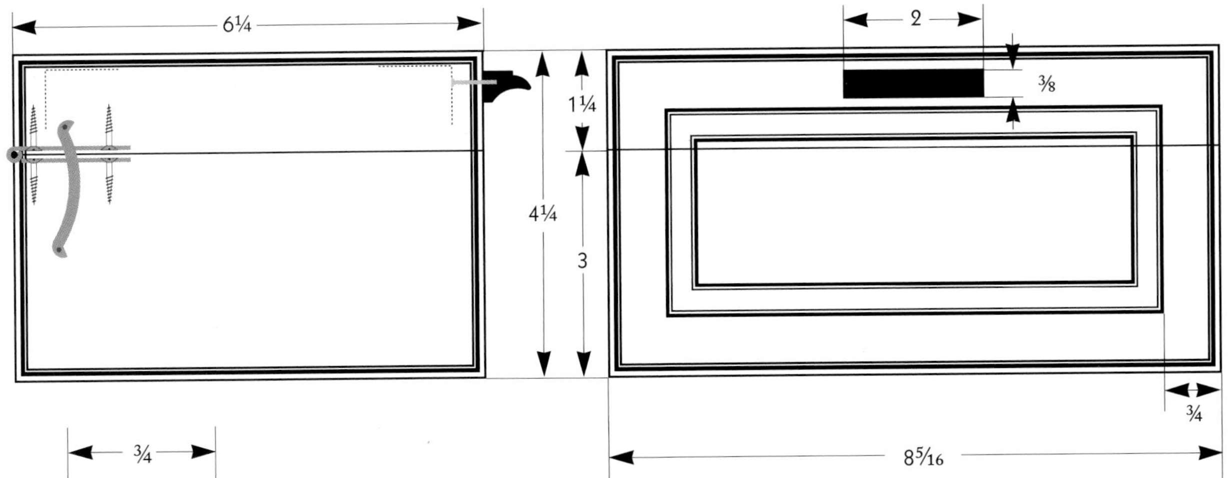
6¼
2
⅜
1¼
4¼
3
¾
8⁵⁄₁₆

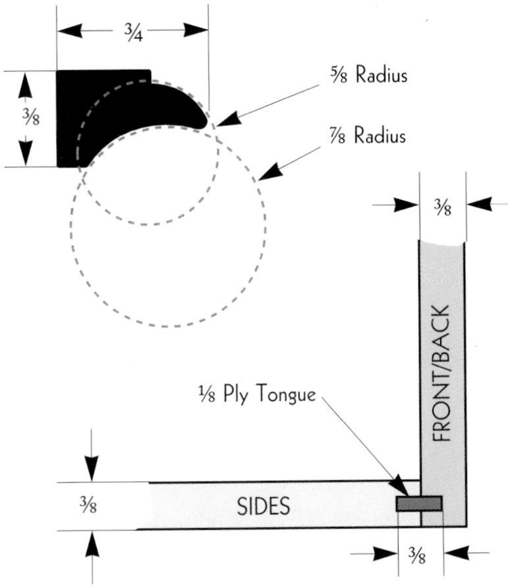
¾
⅜
⅝ Radius
⅞ Radius
⅜
FRONT/BACK
⅛ Ply Tongue
⅜
SIDES
⅜

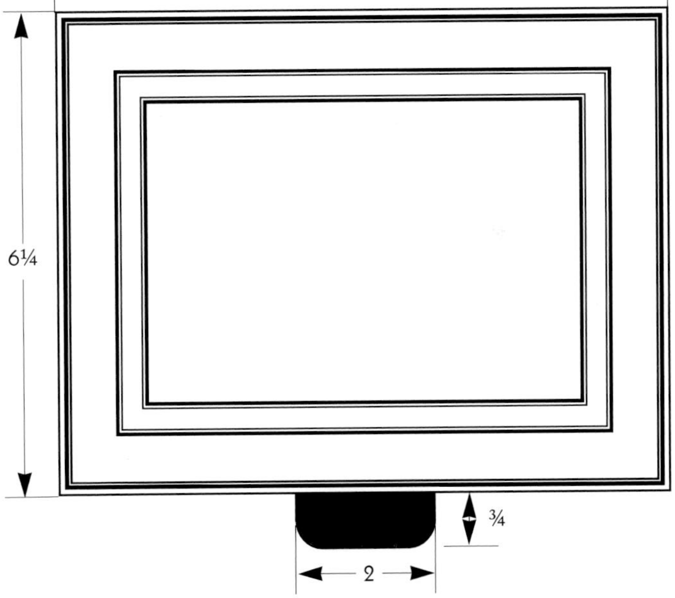
6¼
¾
2

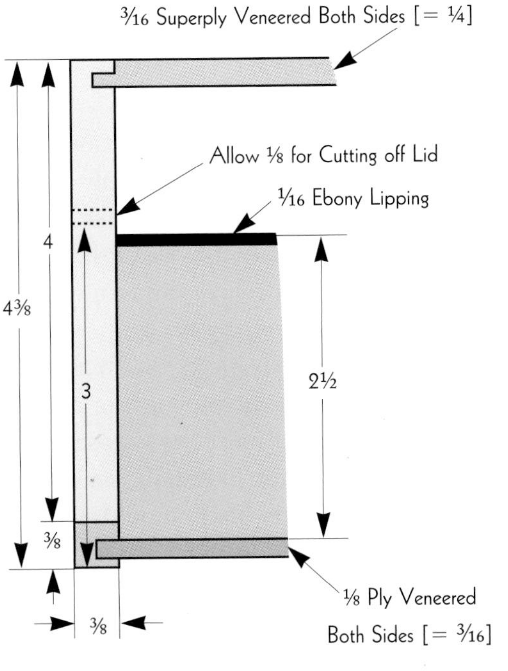
³⁄₁₆ Superply Veneered Both Sides [= ¼]
Allow ⅛ for Cutting off Lid
¹⁄₁₆ Ebony Lipping
4
4⅜
3
2½
⅜
⅜
⅛ Ply Veneered
Both Sides [= ³⁄₁₆]

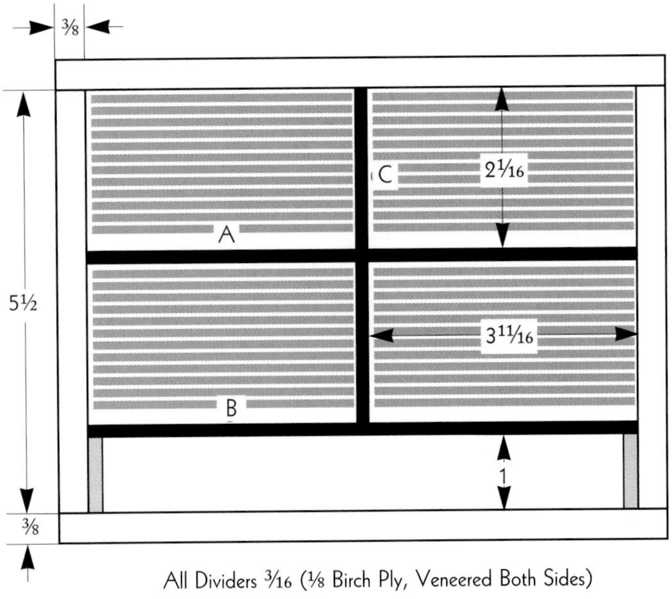
⅜
C
2¹⁄₁₆
A
5½
3¹¹⁄₁₆
B
1
⅜
All Dividers ³⁄₁₆ (⅛ Birch Ply, Veneered Both Sides)

ELEMENT	MATERIAL	QTY	LENGTH	X x Y
BOX SIDES/	⅜" Birch Ply	2	5½" *	4"
FRONT & BACK	⅜" Birch Ply	2	8⁵⁄₁₆" *	4"
"	Maple	2	5½" *	⅜" x ⅜" *
"	Maple	2	8⁵⁄₁₆"	⅜" x ⅜" *
LID	¹⁄₁₆" Birch Ply	3	8⁵⁄₁₆"	6¼"
BASE	⅛" Birch Ply	1	8⁵⁄₁₆"	6¼"
DIVIDERS	⅛" Birch Ply	2	7⁹⁄₁₆" *	2½"
	⅛" Birch Ply	1	4⁹⁄₁₆" *	2½"
	Ebony	2	7⁹⁄₁₆" *	³⁄₃₂" x ³⁄₁₆"
	Ebony	1	4⁹⁄₁₆" *	³⁄₃₂" x ³⁄₁₆"
HANDLE	Ebony	1	5"	⅜" x ¾"

■ **Colored Lines** You can buy ready made lines for this project if you like, but the vast majority of lines available are made from natural woods and suitable only if you are doing traditional style work—it is far better to make up your own. See how to do this in Project 3, the Jewelry Box.

When placing the decorative lines around the edges of a box, these can either be the same distance from the outer edges all the way round or you can take into consideration the proportional difference between the length and depth of the box—that is, the lines will be further from the ends than from the front and back. As a general rule, the nearer you want them to be to the outside edge, the more they should tend towards being an equal distance from that edge all round. The nearer to the center you want them to be, the more they should tend towards the proportional approach, otherwise the resulting rectangle will tend towards completely different proportions to the surrounding box. For this project I have used both approaches—the first way for the exterior lines and the second way for the lines inside the lid, as they form a much smaller panel.

■ **Hinges** This can be a very tricky task. The method I set out here is a safe, reliable and reasonably quick way to achieve a neat result. I use the router to set the exact depth of the cut and to remove most of the waste—then the exact shape and dimensions of each hinge are cut in separately by hand.

■ **Choosing Veneer** The four pieces that make up the main box need to be veneered on the inside before the box is constructed, and I have chosen fiddle-back maple for the interior. In order to maintain stability, both sides of each piece should be veneered, and I have used the least figured sections from the same leaves for this "balancing."

ELEMENT	MATERIAL	QTY	LENGTH	X x Y
VENEERS				
INTERIOR/ FRONT & BACK	Figured Maple (Good)	2	8¾" *	4¾" *
"	Figured Maple (Balance)	2	8¾" *	4¾" *
SIDES	Figured Maple (Good)	2	6" *	4¾" *
"	Figured Maple (Balance)	2	6" *	4¾" *
LID & BASE	Figured Maple (Good)	2	8⁵⁄₁₆" *	6¼" *
"	Figured Maple (Balance)	2	8⁵⁄₁₆" *	6¼" *
EXTERIOR/ FRONT & BACK	Steamed Figured Maple	2	8¾"	4¾"
SIDES	Steamed Figured Maple	2	6¾"	4¾"
INNER EDGES	Steamed Figured Maple	1	6¾"	2"
"	Steamed Figured Maple	1	8¾"	2"
LID	Steamed Figured Maple	1	8¾"	6¾"
DECORATIVE LINES:				
CURVED	Dyed Veneers	8 approx.	16½"	¾" *
B/B/W/B	Bought or Homemade	-	11' approx.	
BOXWOOD		-	7' approx.	⅛" square
DECORATIVE	Bought or Homemade	-	5' approx.	
PLUS:	Quadrant hinges and screws			

The exterior is steamed Canadian maple. Carefully choose a nicely figured bit for the back, better bits for the sides, a really beautiful bit for the front and for the lid. There should be a well defined hierarchy: back, sides, front, and lid in ascending order of importance. Each face is made up of a single piece of veneer divided at the lid margin.

■ *Finish* If you intend to French polish this box, refer to the section on French polishing, on pages 16 to 20, before you begin.

1

2

3

4

5

6

Veneering the Interior

1. Veneer a piece of ⅛" birch plywood and a piece of "SuperPly" (refer to Project 2, the Backgammon Board), each 8¼" x 6¼", with figured maple on both sides—use the very best figured piece for inside the lid. When dry, sand thoroughly and give both sides of the base and the interior of the lid a coat of thinned shellac sanding sealer (SSS) to seal them and protect the light color. When dry, apply a further full-strength coat of SSS to the interior surfaces of each piece and set aside.

Saw the birch ply and maple to the dimensions shown in the plan.

2. Allow about ¹⁄₁₆″ overlength, plane the edges of the maple which will be glued, and glue it to the ply, holding it firmly in place with masking tape.

When dry, remove the tape and plane the pieces flush.

3. Veneer the pieces with the figured maple on one side and the less figured maple on the other for balance.

When dry, trim off excess veneer and plane exactly square and to length, and give the inner faces only a coat of thinned SSS.

Preparing the Sides for Assembly

4. Now set up the router with a ⅛" straight cutter, cut a groove ³⁄₁₆" deep in a piece of scrap, and test a piece of ⅛" ply in the groove to check for a snug, push fit. If satisfied, set up a high fence (at least 3") slightly more than ⅛" from the near corner of the cutter. Cut a groove centrally in the end of each side piece, passing them through, on end, with the outside face held against the high fence.

Then pass the pieces for front and back through with the inside faces downwards. These grooves should continue out of the top edges of these pieces but stop ³⁄₁₆" short of their bottom (lipped) edges—mark the fence for safety. Cut some ⅜"-wide strips of the ⅛" birch ply, 3¹⁵⁄₁₆" long, and check that the box goes together neatly. If it doesn't, you may have to sand/plane the strips slightly until the pieces go together easily.

5. Now remove the veneer from the inside ends of front and back where the sides will be glued: assemble each corner in turn, cut along with a sharp scalpel, as shown, and remove with a chisel.

6. Cut the ³⁄₁₆" grooves to take the lid and the base and the lid cut-off groove. All grooves can be taken full length on the sides but must be stopped ³⁄₁₆" short of the ends of the front and back. Cut the rabbet around the upper edge of the lid.

7. Assemble the box to check that everything is going together as it should. If all is fine, disassemble and cut the inside half of the ⅛" lid cut-off groove ³⁄₁₆" deep and leave the router set up. Finally, give both sides of the base and the inner faces of the front, back, and sides another coat of SSS and set aside to dry.

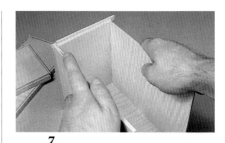

7

Fitting the Decorative Lines inside the Lid

8. Take some pieces of your chosen line, lay them out on the inside of the lid panel, and decide exactly how far you want to set them in from the edge. Read through the introduction to this project again, on pages 22 and 24. See especially the section on "Colored Lines," on page 24. When you have decided, stick some masking tape around the edges and mark to show the exact positions of your lines.

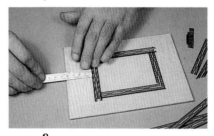

8

Make a small square ended scraper from a piece of hacksaw blade the exact width of your line. Hold a straightedge along the outside of where you want your first line to be and scrape along it to score the veneer, particularly to mark where the inner edge of the line will be with the far edge of the scraper. Keep the straightedge in place and make a scalpel cut along the outside of the line, and then place the straightedge along the inside of the scored mark and make another scalpel cut along its inner edge.

9

9. Repeat for all four sides, being particularly careful that the external corners are neatly worked and none of the lines overrun, and remove the waste with a chisel.

10

10. Now cut pieces of your chosen line to length, fit them into your prepared channels, and carefully miter the corners as you go. If you find that any of the pieces are a little tight, you can thin them slightly by sanding their edges gently on abrasive paper. Glue in each piece as soon as you have gotten it to fit perfectly. When all the lines are fitted, set aside to dry.

11

11. When dry, bring the lines down flush, first by chiseling, and then by scraping. The chisel must be very sharp for this, to avoid pulling up any of the fibers of the dyed veneers which tend to be quite soft and fibrous.

12. Give the surface a good dusting, and then apply two coats of shellac sanding sealer, allowing it to dry between. When completely dry, smooth the inner surface of this and both sides of the base with 1200-grit wet and dry and 0000 wire wool.

12

13

14

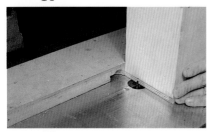

15

16

17

18

Assembly

13. Smooth both sides of the base and the inner faces of front, back and sides with 1200 wet & dry and 0000 wire wool, and wax all your finished surfaces with a good quality clear furniture wax, buff, and remove any wax and finish from the glue areas around the lid and base.

14. As usual, do a dry run: assemble the pieces clamped down onto the bench as shown and, if satisfied, do it for real with glue checking that it is going together absolutely square.

15. When dry, sand the corners flush and cut the lid off on the router (which is still hopefully set up as you left it). Don't go quite full depth but leave about ¹⁄₆₄" and cut this through with a scalpel. Remove any slivers from the raw edges, and then plane and sand the inner edges smooth and level with the aid of a blinde-ended sanding board (see the description in the section "Useful Jigs & Aids," page 13) until lid and box fit together perfectly. Also check that both sides, front and back are completely flush, and if not, correct by scraping and/or sanding. Sand the lid absolutely level, making sure that the edges are not proud. I have used a little bit of filler on the lid to fill in a couple of minor unevennesses. Dust thoroughly when satisfied.

Veneering the Exterior

Choose your veneer carefully, one piece for each side, one each for back and front, one for the lid, and two further pieces, 6¾" x 2" and 8½" x 2", to yield the inner edges, and mark each with chalk or faint pencil so you know which is which. Cut all pieces at least ½" oversize in both dimensions.

16. Cut four strips from each of the pieces for the inner edges, ½" wide, and veneer these two at a time to the lid and box, applying pressure in the veneer press or with clamps, rigid boards and lengths of angle iron. Start with the long edges and use 10 percent diluted PVA brushed on evenly, placing a piece of paper, a piece of carpet underlay, and finally a rigid board on top.

17. When dry, carefully cut the miters at the corners of the veneered pieces, then miters to match on the shorter pieces, and veneer these in place too with the corners held together with veneer tape.

18. Trim the veneer flush around all edges very carefully with a fresh scalpel. If you will be inlaying the B/W/B line around the inner edges, it is best to veneer these pieces so that they do not quite reach the inner edge of the box.

19. Now veneer the lid: The inside needs to be supported with some pieces of scrap cut to just less than the internal dimensions but slightly higher so that the edges of the lid are not quite on the setting up board. You must place a piece of mount card or something similarly protective immediately under the inside of the lid, and make sure it is completely free of dust and dirt before you put the lid under any pressure, otherwise you can seriously damage your carefully inlaid design! Apply the diluted pva and brush out evenly, put the veneer in place, add paper, underlay and board, and put in the press.

19

20. All other surfaces are basically veneered in the same way except that the pieces for the sides are cut into two first. Mark a straight, square line down the inside of one end of the first piece and mark a line square to this where the lid margin will be (these pieces are a little oversized—share this between the two pieces), and make the cut. Mark each piece (L, R, B, F, etc.) above and below the lid line and cut them apart.

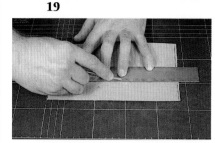

20

21. Clamp the box on its edge down onto the workbench and veneer as before, applying glue and making sure that the line you drew at one end lines up exactly with the end of the box. Then when you veneer the top half, the figure will line up exactly. Apply paper, underlay and board as before, clamping around the side of the box, and remember to protect the interior.

21

After you have veneered each face, trim off the excess veneer before you go on to veneer the next bit. Continue until you have veneered all exterior surfaces.

22. Sand all surfaces thoroughly, dust, and apply a couple of coats of full-strength SSS.

22

Decoration

Notice that the curved lines appear to flow under the straight, colored lines but over the BB/W/B and boxwood squares at the very edges of the box. The order in which I have inlaid the lines here is important if you want to achieve this effect. The external decoration gets applied in the following order: BBWB lines, boxwood squares, wavy lines (having first cut out the slightly undersized channels for the straight, colored lines), and then, finally, the colored lines.

23

23. First tape the box together securely with 1" masking tape.

24. Fit the BB/W/B lines and boxwood squares all around every edge—see how to do this in Project 4, Henry's Christening Box, especially pages 67 through 71.

24

25

26

27

28

29

30

25. Now decide exactly where you want the straight colored lines to go. On this box, they start exactly ¾" in from the outside edge; this allows a reasonable amount of the alternative colored wavy lines to show on the lid before they "drop" over the sides. Use a router cutter that is about ⅛" smaller than the width of your chosen line. Set the fence so that you are cutting a channel in the middle of where you want the line, that is, leaving about ¹⁄₃₂" on either side to be trimmed by hand.

26. Cut out the majority of the waste by making incomplete passes, stopping just short of each corner—these will be worked by hand later. Use marks made on tape stuck along the top of your fence to indicate where each pass should start and stop. The box will need to be carefully lowered onto the cutter at the beginning of each pass and lifted off at the end. Work slowly and steadily, holding the box gently but firmly against the fence. Work the lid and front in this way.

Making the Wavy Lines

27. First cut a wavy line freehand along a piece of ¾" mdf, 2½" x 16", and cut some strips of dyed veneer to create the color scheme you require ½" longer than your form and fractionally wider.

28. Use watered-down pva (about 90 percent glue to 10 percent water) and work quite quickly because as the glue dries the strips can start to curl up and become difficult to control.

29. When you have applied glue to the strips and they are satisfactorily stacked, clamp them up in the form using small C clamps.

30. When this is dry—after about two hours—unclamp all except two of the clamps and use the form to hold the sandwich while you plane one side of it true and flat. Make sure that you keep the clamps below the level of the top of the form, otherwise you will get a chipped plane iron! Keep planing until you get a couple of complete, unbroken shavings, remove from the form, and you are ready to saw off the lines for inlaying. If you are using two different color schemes as I did here, make up your second sandwich now.

31. Cut the strips off using a small bandsaw with as fine a blade as you can find. You are bound to lose a substantial amount of your sandwich as dust, but the finer the blade the less you will lose. Set up a fence high enough to support the block on its side (see notes on using small band saws, page 10—they are particularly relevant for this operation) and cut slices about ¹⁄₃₂" thick. This will allow the lines to go in a little proud of the surrounding veneer, ready for trimming flush after all the inlaying has been done.

32. After you have cut off each line, plane the saw marks from the edge again—this planed side is the one that gets glued down.

Fitting the Wavy Lines

33. Now spend a little time "playing" with the wavy lines! Start with the center panel, experimenting to see what works. Although you have made all your lines in the same form, there should be enough variation within each complete length to give the impression of random curves. Don't be afraid to cut a section out of the middle of a line to get at that bit that curves in just the right way.

34. Each piece needs to be undercut slightly so that the cross section is "boat-shaped." Do this by using a curved sanding block—here I used a small plastic pot with some 180-grit garnet stuck to it. Tape the first piece into position, as shown. These pieces are surprisingly rigid and resistant to lateral bending—one piece of tape near to each end (and perhaps one in the center for a long piece) should hold the piece securely.

35. Gently mark around the piece with a sharp scalpel, twisting the blade slightly to follow accurately the curves of the piece. The handle should be tipped away from the piece slightly so that the tip of the blade is following the bottom of the piece, that is, the narrowest part. This is important because when you mark around a piece with the scalpel and then reinforce these cuts to the full depth of the veneer, the thickness of the scalpel blade tends to widen the channel slightly, and this undercutting ensures that the pieces fit snugly into place.

36. Carefully reinforce the cuts, starting gently, being careful that you don't deviate from the correct line. As when making the initial marking with the piece in place, you will need to keep the direction of the scalpel cut exactly in line with the curve you are cutting—that means that the angle of the blade will need to be constantly changing. Progress to a firmer pressure to cut to the full depth of the veneer and remove the waste with a narrow chisel. Test your piece in place—it is unlikely to be too loose but it could be a little tight in places—slightly increase the undercutting at these areas using the curved block until the fit is perfect. Don't try to widen the channel you have cut out—this is asking for trouble! These lines should fit into place to the full depth of the veneer and be glued to the bottom of the recess cut for them, otherwise they can pop up later when you are doing the final leveling. When you are satisfied with the fit, apply a small amount of glue, spread evenly, and push the line into place—no clamping or other applied pressure should be necessary. Repeat for all other lines in the central panel.

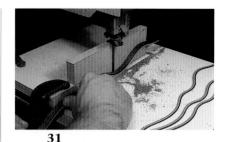

31

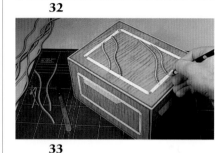

32

33

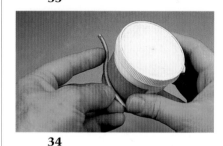

34

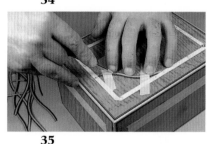

35

36

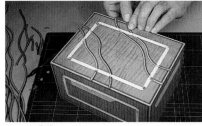

37

38

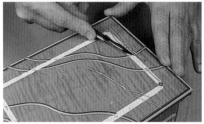

39

40

41

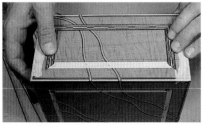

42

37. Now have another play with the next bits of these lines that continue right up to the edges of the lid. Ensure that the curves of the new pieces appear to continue smoothly from the pieces already in place. It is best that these short pieces should meet the edge of the lid at something approaching 90 degrees, otherwise the joining with the vertical pieces is very difficult to do neatly. Allow just enough length to protrude into the channels as before and just over the lid edges. When satisfied, mark their exact positions, which is which, and proceed to fit as before.

38. Continue working in this way down the back, both sides, and then the front. The box is still taped together at this stage, and the only difference with this part of the job is that you inlay each line in a single piece across the lid margin but don't actually glue it into place. Start by trimming the top end of each piece so that it fits snugly in under the end of each of the lines still overhanging the lid edge. When you have inlaid the lines as before and achieved a neat fit (unglued), place the straightedge exactly along the margin line and make a gentle cut with a scalpel, precisely where you need to divide the piece. Remove it and finish the cut, not with the scalpel, but with a sharp chisel, held vertically, and with the end of the piece overhanging the end of a block so that when the chisel digs into the piece the overhanging bit droops down. This avoids the thickness of the chisel crushing and compressing the end of the line. This is important because doing it this way you don't have any spare line to trim back! Glue the pieces in place with a piece of waxed paper in the lid margin to avoid gluing the lid to the box!

39. When all curved lines are fitted, trim them flush with the surrounding veneer with careful chiseling. It is not necessary to achieve an absolutely level surface at this stage—this will be done when the straight lines have been fitted.

Fitting the Straight Lines

40. Now cut round the outside and inside of each partially cut channel for the lines on the lid and front, cutting firmly with a scalpel against a straightedge chopping off the spare ends of the curved lines and widening to take your lines.

41. Carefully complete the outer corners, being careful not to overrun with any of your cuts, and remove the waste with careful chiseling or with a scalpel.

42. Fit the lines as you did inside the lid—the only difference being that you will have to divide the vertical lines on the front as you did with the curved ones.

43. When all lines are fitted, chisel flush, and scrape thoroughly to produce an absolutely level surface—don't sand! Apply two coats of 50 percent SSS and 50 percent transparent French polish, and set aside to dry while you make a cup of tea and have a rest—you have been working hard!

Quadrant Hinges

Mark each hinge so that you know which one is which. First, remove the stay (quadrant) from the hinge by grinding off one of the small retaining lugs. Measure the width of the stay arm, subtract this from the thickness of the sides, and add ½32" to this value. Set up the router with a wide straight cutter with the fence exactly this value from the near edge of the cutter.

44. The cutting depth should be exactly half the thickness of your hinges at the pin—test this carefully on pieces of scrap first until you have a perfect fit, as shown. Err on the side of being shallow, but it is best to get this exactly right the first time.

45. Measure the length of the stay arm from the center of the pin and mark, on a piece of tape fixed along the fence, this value less about ⅟16" from each opposite corner of the cutter. It is advisable, particularly with highly figured or crumbly veneers, to make cuts with a scalpel, as shown, to stop the veneer breaking away—these should be made between where the furthest edge of all cuts will be and the final edges of the recesses.

46. When satisfied that the router is set up correctly, switch on and move the back of the lid, with the side against the fence, onto the cutter just as far as the mark on the fence. Repeat for the other side and then for both sides of the box. Widen the cut to almost the full width of the main back flap of the hinge by adjusting the fence so that the far edge of the cutter is just less than where the inner edge of the hinge will be.

47. When you have opened out the recesses on the lid and base you then need to enlarge them by hand to take your hinges exactly.

48. Carefully trim the recess for the stay arm exactly to width. Do this with a small straightedge and a scalpel, as shown, until the inner edge of the stay arm is flush with the lid's inner edge, and then cut the end square and to length so that the front of the main flap is flush with the inner back edge. Now trim the back edge of the recess to take the full width of the main back flap of the hinge by making careful, vertical cuts with a wide chisel until the hinge just drops into place. Repeat this process so that you have neat-fitting recesses for all four flaps.

43

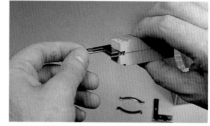

44

45

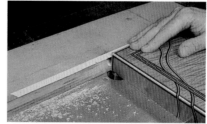

46

47

48

49

50

51

52

53

54

49. With each hinge in place make a mark centrally at each end of the cutaway for the stays, remove the hinges, and make a further mark in each recess about ¹⁄₁₆" further back on the same line. Drill these out (to take the stays when the box is shut) using a ¼" "lip and spur" drill bit. Drill good and deep down into the main box (the full length of the stays) but less deep in the lid. It is safest to do these holes using a drill press/stand in order to minimize the possibility of breaking through into the interior of the box.

50. You will then need to join your holes up with chiseling, and to generally clean up these holes so that the hinges, with stays inserted, fit and function freely.

51. Drill and fit the hinges in place in the lid using all screws. Fit this in place using one screw only per hinge to the main box. If box and lid line up perfectly then drill all other holes dead center and fit screws. If it doesn't line up (much more likely) then drill one of the remaining holes on each side slightly offset in the direction you want the lid to move—common sense should suggest the fine detail of this. Continue adjusting until you have achieved perfection.

If at any stage you find that things are going horribly wrong, and the lid and base are nowhere near matching up, you may well have to plug some, or even all, of the holes you have already made. See Project 10, Olly's Chinese Balls, for how to deal with a problem such as this.

The screws you have used to fit the hinges at this stage should not be the ones you finally use—see the section on "Cleaning Up Hardware," pages 20 and 21.

Fitting the Line Around the Interior

52. If you have decided that you are going to fit this line, now is the time to do it. I have chosen a ready made B/W/B line about ¹⁄₁₆" wide. Remove the hinges and use the purfling cutter to gently mark the veneer at each end of the inner edge of both sides on lid and base and at both ends and in the middle for front and back (this is just in case there is any slight distortion along the front or back). This should be at a distance to allow for an extra sliver of the veneer to be removed just before you glue the line in place.

53. Now use a scalpel and straightedge to join these marks up.

54. Very carefully remove the waste with a sharp chisel. This must be done very carefully, ensuring that you don't remove any more than just the thickness of the veneer. When you have satisfactorily removed this waste, you must now trim back the lines so that the recesses take your individual bits of line exactly.

These lines do vary slightly in width—bought ready made and even (or especially!) homemade—and it is best to adapt individual pieces for this particular job as you will not be able to do any cleaning off of the inside edge because the interior of the box has already been finished. You can do a bit of sanding, very carefully, to remove any glue, but you want to keep this to an absolute minimum.

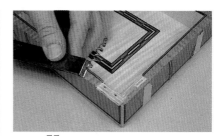

55

Start with the back edge and work counterclockwise around the box, and then the lid, carefully widening the recesses and mitring the corners as you go. Don't use too much glue; only a little is necessary for this job. You will find that these lines do not need to be taped down—the stickiness of the glue will hold them very well. Just push them firmly into place and they will stay.

55. When the glue is dry, which will be very quick for this job, carefully trim the lines down to the level of the surrounding veneer. This is best done using a wide chisel, as shown—you could carefully use a scraper if you need to, but this should not be necessary. Give the inside edges a coat of sanding sealer.

56

Now either smooth and wax all surfaces or French polish—see the section on French polishing, pages 16 through 20, which uses this box as its example.

56. Rout a piece of ebony ¾" x ⅜" x 5" to the profile in the plan—use whatever cutters you have available to arrive at a similar profile. Cut a piece 2" long from it (the rest will come in handy for future projects), round over the corners as show in the plan, sand smooth, and apply a coat of thinned SSS.

57

57. When dry, sand smooth, wax and screw in place from inside the lid—I have used small, countersunk brass machine screws.

58. Cut the dividers slightly oversize from ⅛" birch ply, veneer both sides with figured maple, sand thoroughly, apply SSS, and set aside to dry. Lip the top edges with ebony, plane flush, and apply another coat of shellac sanding sealer. Trim the pieces exactly to size—this assembly should fit loosely in the box so that, eventually, the box can have other uses.

58

59. Cut half slots in each of pieces A and C, one from the top and one from the bottom, as shown.

59

60. Each piece should fit snugly into the other. Cut a two-thirds-depth groove down the middle of the back of piece B to take the front end of piece C. Smooth all pieces and glue together. This assembly sits in the box held in position with a couple of small maple blocks wedged in between the bottom front corners and piece B—these will hold the assembly in place perfectly well.

60

2 BACKGAMMON BOARD

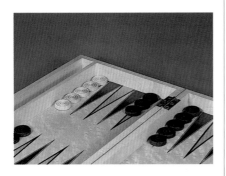

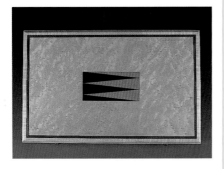

This is a colorful version of the board for this popular game. The size of your pieces will affect the dimensions of your finished board—it is important to make the board section first, and allow this to dictate the exact dimensions of the actual box.

I have used ¼" "SuperPly" for this project—this is ply that I make up myself from ¹⁄₁₆" birch ply, which is available from some timber merchants—it is worth searching for! I use three layers to produce a board that is more rigid and stable, for its thickness and weight, than any other wood product, hence making it ideal for this and many other projects, especially pieces with curved lids. You can use standard ³⁄₁₆" birch ply—get the best quality you can—and you will still be able to make a good board, but my preference would always be to make up my own SuperPly.

You will need to make a template for the shape of the "points." This is best made from brass, as this is least likely to be damaged. However, ¹⁄₁₆" birch ply is an acceptable substitute, if you are careful when you are cutting around it. You will need a clear center marked on the base.

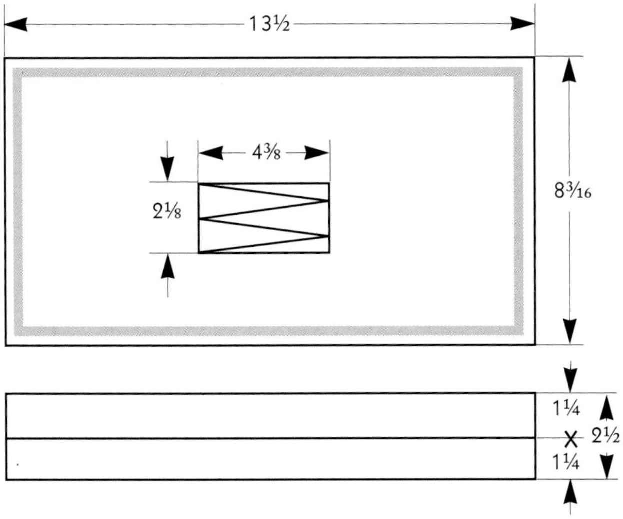
13½
4⅜
2⅛
8³⁄₁₆
1¼
2½
1¼

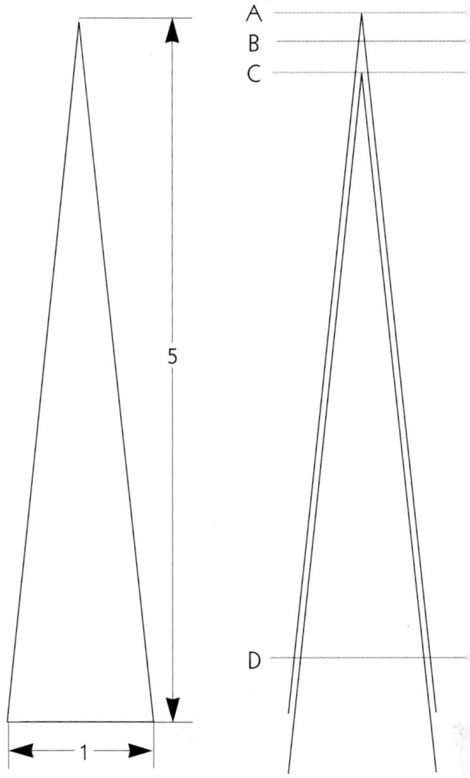
5
1
A
B
C
D

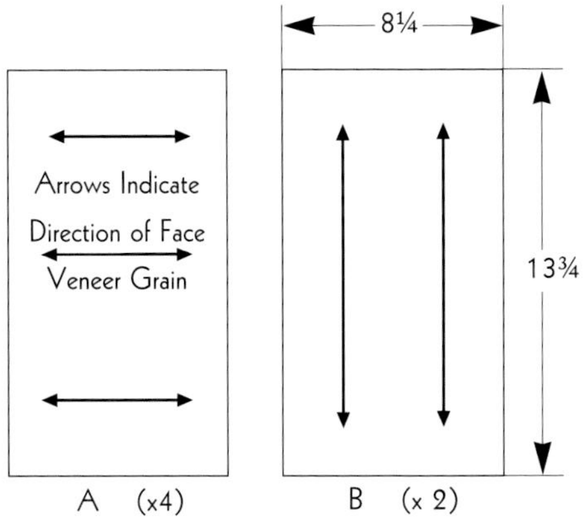
8¼
Arrows Indicate
Direction of Face
Veneer Grain
13¾
A (x4)
B (x 2)

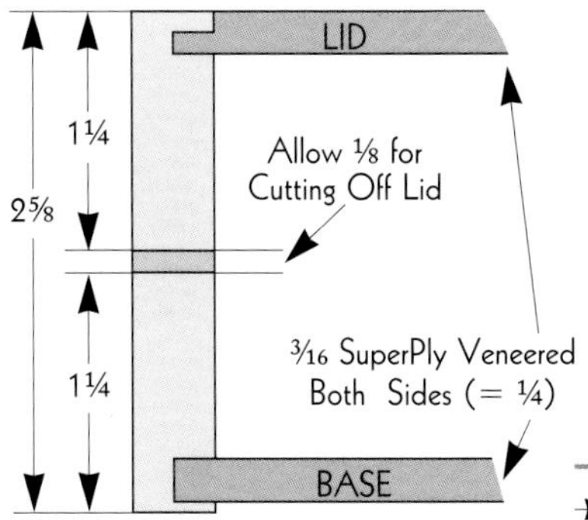
LID
1¼
2⅝
Allow ⅛ for
Cutting Off Lid
1¼
³⁄₁₆ SuperPly Veneered
Both Sides (= ¼)
BASE

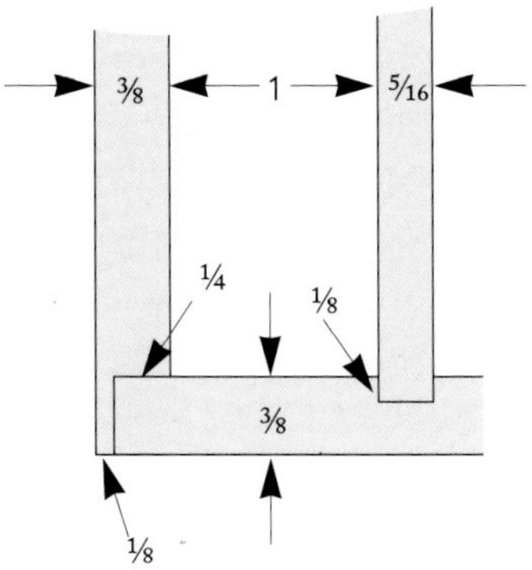
⅜
1
⁵⁄₁₆
¼
⅛
⅜
⅛

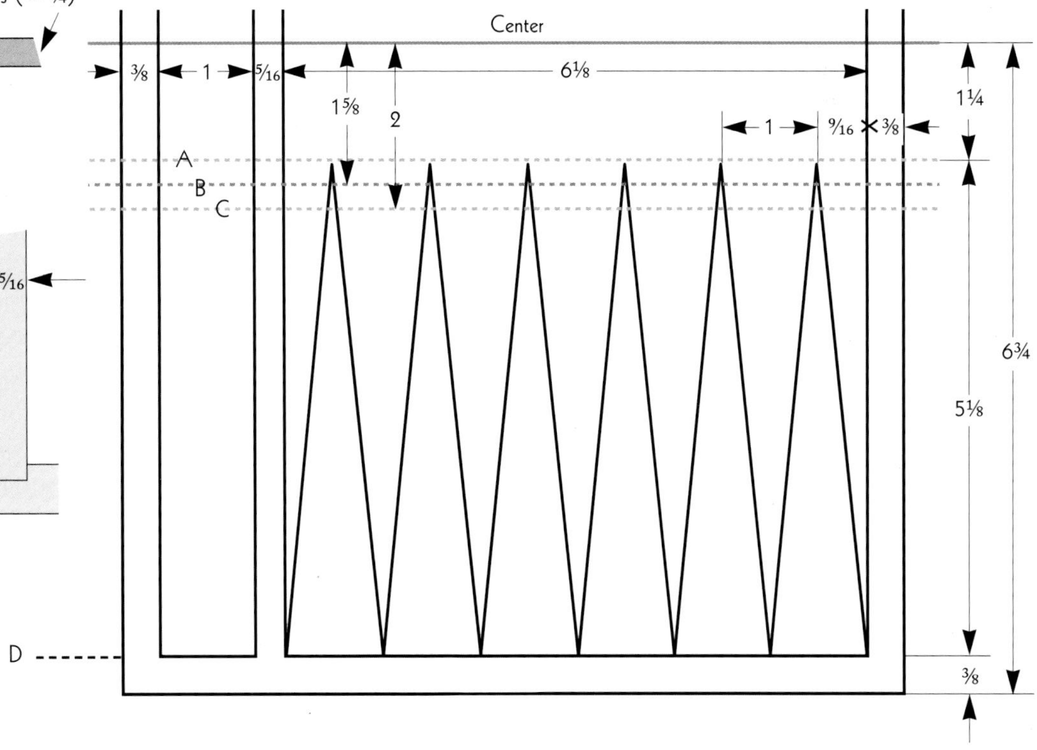
Center
⅜
1
⁵⁄₁₆
6⅛
1⅝
2
1
⁹⁄₁₆
⅜
1¼
A
B
C
6¾
5⅛
D
⅜

ELEMENT	MATERIAL	QTY	LENGTH	X x Y
FRONT & BACK	Maple	2	13½" *	2⅝" x ⅜"
ENDS	Maple	2	7¹⁵⁄₁₆"	2⅝" x ⅜"
DIVIDERS	Maple	2	13" *	¹⁵⁄₁₆" * x ⁵⁄₁₆" *
LID & BASE	¹⁄₁₆" Birch Ply	6 §	13¾"	8¼"
VENEERS:				
LID & BASE	Birds Eye Maple	4	13¾"	8¼"
POINTS & LINES	Dyed Veneer Col.	1	18"	6"
	Dyed Veneer Col.	1	18"	6"
	Dyed Veneer Black	1	18"	2"
PLUS:	Butt hinges and screws (& pieces?)			

* A reminder that in all the cutting lists, the asterisk indicates that you should allow a little extra for trimming to length later.
§ You could substitute a single piece of ³⁄₁₆" birch plywood for each.

1

2

Making the Board

1. To make the SuperPly needed for this board, you will need two pieces of mdf or similar, 1" thick, some pieces of angle iron, and some clamps—these need to have at least a 3" opening. If you have a reasonably sized veneer or book press then this will make life much easier. Cut the six pieces of birch ply a little over size, ensuring that you have four pieces with the grain of the face veneer running across (A) and two pieces with the grain running lengthwise (B). Place one piece of the birch ply (A) centrally onto the mdf, with a piece of paper behind it, and tape it into place with masking tape overlapping about ¼" at each end. Now paint on some diluted (10 percent water) pva glue, covering the whole surface evenly. Place the second piece (B) on the first, tape in place, and apply another coat of pva. Now put the third piece in place and put first a piece of paper and then a piece of carpet underlay and the other piece of mdf on top, and put the whole lot in your veneer press or apply your prepared pieces of angle iron and clamps.

Cutting Out the Points

2. First, select your background veneer, and cut your chosen pieces so that they are each a little larger than your prepared board halves. Carefully mark the centerlines along each piece. Draw a line (B) 1⅝" on either side of each centerline. This line (B) defines where the apex of the template is to be placed for the initial cutting out. Refer to the plan to see the placement and identification of the various lines needed to lay out the board design.

3. Now mark six lines at each end of each board half, at 90 degrees to line B and 1" apart—allow 9⁄16" at each end. Refer to the plan to see the spacing and placement.

4. Now proceed to cut out the points by cutting around the template with a sharp scalpel or craft knife. Absolute accuracy is not essential at this stage as there will be the colored line inlaid along all the joins.

5. Once you have used the template to cut out the points from both opposite ends of each piece of veneer, you should have cut out 24 points.

6. Then take the veneer pieces in your selected colors and cut the points to fit in the spaces you have just cut. Use the same template to cut out 12 points in each of the two colors you have chosen.

7. Now the points need to be edge-glued into place. Put a little full-strength pva on the end of a finger and run the finger along the edge of the piece of veneer. Try this on a piece of scrap first, especially if you are not familiar with this gluing technique. This way you will see how the veneer picks up just the right amount of glue from your finger.

8. Tape the points in position using low-tack masking tape or veneer tape. I suggest that you proceed in gluing and taping down these points with no more than three or four points at a time. Then you should take the taped-up section, and place it in the veneer press—or in the mdf/clamp set-up—to make sure that the pieces glue up completely flush.

You do not need much pressure or you will weld the masking tape to the veneer, and then you will not be able to remove it without taking some of the veneer with it or leaving a gummy residue on the veneer that it is very difficult to remove. Remember to alternate the colors, and make sure that the bottom left point is always the same color—refer to the plan to see exactly how the points should be arranged. Repeat this process of gluing, taping, and gently pressing until you have inserted all of your points.

3

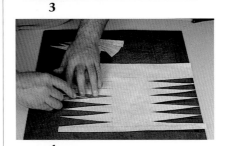

4

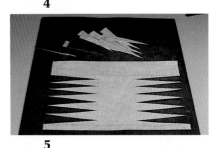

5

6

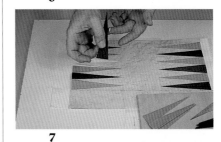

7

8

9

10

11

12

13

Veneering the Board Halves

9. Carefully remove the tape from the front of your prepared pieces, and the paper from the back. Cut two further pieces of the same background veneer for the other sides of the board—that is, the outside of the box. Tape the external veneer, face down, on your setting-up board, with a piece of paper underneath, and tape it in place.

10. Apply the thinned pva to this, then the SuperPly board and then your prepared playing surface. It is not essential to do any accurate lining up at this stage as the veneered board will be squared up later in relation to the design on it—remember, everything is a little oversized at this stage. Repeat for the other half of the board.

Making the Colored Lines

Veneers are laminated together to form a plank, and thin slivers are cut off the edge. You will need 48 pieces of this narrow colored line, 6" long, 24 each of purple and orange.

11. Start by making a template out of scrap card or similar material, 6¼" x 3¼", and use it to cut around to produce four pieces of black veneer and two each of purple and orange. The grain should run parallel to the long sides of these pieces.

12. To make the orange line, take one piece of the black veneer and tape it down onto a setting-up board with a piece of paper behind it. Apply tape along the ends of a second black piece and both orange pieces so that they are ready to lay down. Brush some thinned pva onto the taped down black piece and tape an orange piece over it—repeat with the second orange piece and finally with the second black piece. Now place a piece of paper over this, a piece of carpet underlay and a firm board and put this into the veneer press or apply your angle irons and clamps. Leave for about an hour.

13. While this is setting, prepare the pieces for the purple lines, and, when set, remove the orange plank from the press and replace with the new purple set-up. Cut off the taped ends from the orange plank and plane both long edges true and square. Repeat this for the purple line when that is ready.

14. Set up the band saw to remove neat, ⅟₃₂" slivers from the long edges of these prepared planks. Cut a line off each long edge of a plank and then plane these edges again, saw off again, and so on. Continue until you have 24 pieces of each color and a few spares, each with a planed surface and a rough sawn surface. The planed surface is glued into the channel; the rough one is smoothed when the line is brought level with the rest of the veneer.

Now repeat this to produce the line for the lid border. I have used: two black, two orange, two purple, two orange and two black. This plank, of course, needs to be long enough to go the full length of the box but only wide enough to produce four lines.

Inlaying the Lines around the Points

I prefer to do this first by scraping, cutting with a sharp scalpel, then removing the waste with a narrow chisel. First, prepare a scraper from an old piece of hacksaw blade exactly the width of your line, and with perfectly square shoulders and end. On each end of each half of the board, draw a line ⅜" in from the end of the points—refer to the plan, line A. This defines where the point of your template is placed.

15. Position the template—your scraper should scrape approximately half on the background veneer and half on the edge of the colored point. Carefully draw the scraper, tilting it forward about 30° from vertical in the direction of travel, until you have a clear impression in the wood of exactly where the line will be. Be careful not to scrape beyond the template; the actual point is cut later with a scalpel. Do this to both sides of the point, and then, holding the template firmly, take your scalpel and cut the near edge of the line, gently at first, then more strongly, taking the cut to the top end of the point, and repeat on the other side of the template.

16. Now, remove the template and place a straightedge so that it is along the outside edge of one channel, facing in, and make a cut there with the scalpel, reinforcing the mark left by the scraper. Repeat for the opposite side of the point. You should now have a clean, scalpel-cut line around both sides of the two channels.

17. Remove the waste with a narrow chisel. If you have made up your own SuperPly, it is best to remove the waste from these channels down to and including the first layer of the ply—this way, the slivers of background and colored veneer come away together, cleanly, in one piece. It is possible to do this whole operation just by scraping and, indeed, this is the traditional way it would have been done, but it can lead to tearing the veneer if the scraper is not kept absolutely pristine, particularly on highly figured or dry, crumbly veneers—and the point area needs to be cut separately in any case. Repeat for all 24 points!

18. You will need to make a small jig to cut the shallow angles at the ends of the lines where they meet at the points. Do this by gluing a scrap of ply or similar material on the top of a small block at the correct angle (half that at the apex of your point template).

14

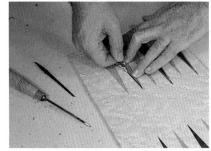

15

16

17

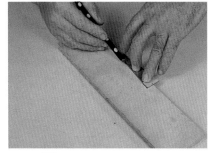

18

19

20

21

22

23

19. This way you can place your piece of line on the block against the ply and plane along the edge to produce the desired angle at the end. It is preferable to cut the end of the piece roughly to the right angle first—see the plan. Trim all your pieces using this jig—half of each color with the planed side up and half with the sawn side up.

The pieces of line should now fit neatly into place in their channels. If there are any tight areas where the line will not sit down in the channel, the line should be slightly undercut. This is best done by holding the line on its edge on the bench and scraping gently with a scalpel held at a slight angle to produce a slightly tapered cross-section along the portion that is tight. This will ensure that you have a really snug fit.

Glue all the pieces in place—remembering to use the opposite color to that of the point you are working on—and keep going until you have done all 24 points!

20. When you have done this, carefully trim the lines down so that they are flush with the surrounding veneer. This is best done by careful planing with a sharp, finely set plane.

21. Then finish off using a sharp cabinet scraper, being sure never to scrape exactly across the grain—this can result in major damage. Work gently and methodically over the whole area, until you have a perfectly level, smooth surface and you have removed all the pencil marks. Don't sand the lines flush—you will just end up with a muddy mess!

22. Once you have a completely clean, smooth surface, scrape and sand the reverse sides of the two board halves, and then apply two or three coats of shellac sanding sealer. The inside could at this stage be French-polished or two-part lacquered. My intention is to gently smooth back the sanding sealer and wax—but there are many different ways this could be finished and I will leave it to personal preference which way you choose. It is important to note that a good general rule is to treat both sides of a board the same; this reduces the risk of any warping or twisting.

Reduce the Board to Size

23. When your chosen finish is completed you need to mark the internal dimensions of the box onto the prepared board halves. Stick some masking tape around all edges of one board and mark the end of the center line at the hinge edge. Now mark 6⅜" from this to one end and, using a transparent square, draw a line along the hinge edge and one across the end, and repeat for the other end.

24. Measure 7⁹⁄₁₆" along the end lines and join these up to complete the rectangle. Now draw a rectangle around this exactly ³⁄₁₆" bigger all round—repeat for the other board half.

25. It helps this operation if you can see through your masking tape—this will make it easier to position these lines so that your points are neatly placed within the finished box. This may result in your wanting to adjust your overall dimensions slightly. This is fine, but remember—your marking out must be exactly square and the size of the two board halves must be identical. Once you have checked and double-checked, cut off just outside the outer line, and plane down exactly to it.

Making the Box

You must choose your hinges before finally deciding on the thickness of the sides of the main carcass. This needs to be about ¹⁄₃₂" less than the distance from the center of the pin to the outer edge of the flaps. This produces a small gap—around ¹⁄₁₆"—between the two halves when the box is opened flat and will allow it to open fully even on a slightly uneven surface.

Now prepare—or buy ready-prepared—the wood for the four sides of the box. Remembering to adjust these dimensions if you have made any alteration to your internal measurements.

26. Now the two ends of the two longer pieces for the front and back need to have the pieces removed from them to form the ½ lap joints that hold the box together. This is a simple joint as it only involves work to half of the pieces but allows a high glue area and is easy to work by hand or by router if mounted on a table. I will assume that you have one!

You will need a sharp, square cutter, ½" or larger and some form of jig to keep the pieces you are working on at 90° to the fence (see "Useful Jigs & Aids," pages 12 and 13). Set up to make a cut ¼" high x ³⁄₈" deep. If you are using hard maple, you will find this easier to do in two cuts, say, ³⁄₁₆" x ⁵⁄₁₆", and then the full values.

27. Now cut two ⁵⁄₁₆" grooves in the sides, across the grain, 1¼" in from one end of each, to take the two dividers. Either do this on the router table with an incomplete cut with an ⁵⁄₁₆" cutter with bottom cut using a 90-degree fence, or cut out by hand using sharp chisels.

28. The object is to get the pieces ready for gluing up. Whichever way you choose, the main requirements are that the channels extend beyond where the grooves for the lid and base will start, and that they stop before the outer edges of the same grooves.

24

25

26

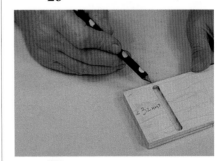
27

28

29

30

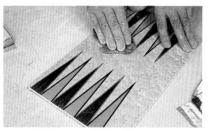

31

32

33

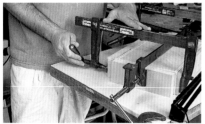

34

A further requirement for each channel is that it must be absolutely square sided, particularly in the middle where the box will ultimately be split in two.

Now cut the series of grooves on each piece as shown on the plan. Check on a scrap first for the fit of the base and, if a ¼" cutter is too loose, use a smaller one and gradually widen the cut using strips of masking tape along the fence. Make sure you still have at least ¹⁄₃₂" at the bottom of the pieces for support.

Cut the groove for the lid to exactly ⅛" and then the rabbet around the lid can be cut to fit the groove. Do this next producing a rabbet ³⁄₁₆" x ⅛" gradually increasing the height of the cut until the lid fits in place snugly.

Finally cut the groove where the box is to be cut open, to a depth of ³⁄₁₆" using a ⅛" cutter—the plan says ³⁄₁₆" but this allows a little bit for cleaning up. Set this operation up so that the cut is as central as possible and make sure you remember which edge—top or bottom—is against the fence because you will now leave the router set up as it is for the actual cutting off after the box has been glued together.

29. Now apply a coat of slightly thinned shellac sanding sealer (SSS) to all inner surfaces. Set aside.

30. When dry, sand gently with 1200-grit wet & dry paper and smooth with 0000 wire wool.

31. Now sand and smooth the playing surfaces.

32. This will take a little longer to arrive at a good, satin finish but it is worth the extra effort.

Do a Dry Run

33. Once you have checked that the box fits together neatly (you may find that you have to plane the edges of the boards a little to achieve this), it is ready for gluing up. It is best to prepare a piece of scrap mdf or similar material for each of the four sides with a piece of ⅝" ply at each end to ensure that pressure is applied exactly where it is needed. I suggest you use one clamp for the ends and two for the back and front.

Gluing up the Box

34. When you are completely happy, apply glue to each end of the pieces for the front and back and along the grooves for top and bottom and clamp up.

When dry, remove the clamps, do any cleaning up to the joints with a plane, and give the sides of the box a good sanding with 180-grit garnet paper.

Now cut the box open on your router set-up if you haven't changed the set-up. If you do need to change it while the box is drying, be sure to make a reference cut on a piece of scrap first. Don't cut the full ³⁄₁₆" depth—⅛" will prevent the box from collapsing—experiment on a short section first.

35. Cut open using a scalpel.

36. Clean up the edges by planing and sanding.

37. A piece of mdf, about 4" x 12", with 180-grit garnet stuck to ⅓ of its length—a blind-ended sanding board—is a very useful tool for leveling edges such as this, using the back end as a guide resting on the opposite edge (see "Useful Jigs & Aids, page 12). Continue until the halves fit together perfectly—and are exactly the same height—especially at the hinge (back) edge so that the board opens completely flat and level.

Fitting the Dividers

Prepare the dividers in this order: length, fit in channel, height.

Arrive at the correct length by planing one edge square, cutting slightly overlength and using a disc sander with a 90° fence or careful planing. Fit to the channel by carefully reducing the thickness of the pieces by planing—one end at a time, mark so that you know which end is which—until each pushes snugly into place. Now plane the height of the piece on a shooting board—not in situ—until it is just right. Glue in place and repeat for the other side.

Fitting the Lid Decoration

38. Your lid will now have an ugly join where the veneered panel meets the solid wood of the box—plane and/or scrape this flush if it isn't already.

Set up the router with a ⁵⁄₃₂" cutter (assuming your line is ³⁄₁₆" wide, as mine is) with the distance from the fence to the near side of the cutter ¹⁄₃₂" less than the minimum distance from the outer edge of the lid to the join. Make an incomplete pass along each edge of the lid, making sure you don't overshoot.

39. Use the scalpel and straightedge to complete the outside corners and to open out the grooves to take your line exactly.

40. Remove the waste.

35

36

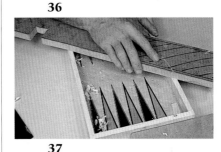

37

38

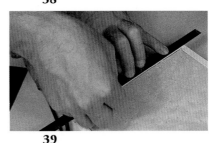

39

40

41

42

43

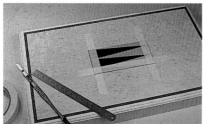

44

45

46

41. Carefully fit the lines in place, cutting neat miters as you go. Be sure to doublecheck each piece for fit before gluing it into place. I find that working in a consistent manner helps me work efficiently and accurately—for instance, I always prefer to work in a counterclockwise direction.

42. Plane and then scrape flush.

Making the Central Decoration

43. Cut out three points of each color using the point template—but only about two-thirds of the full length—and edge-glue these together on a setting-up board in the pattern shown, or in one of your choosing, and put under a little pressure to ensure that they glue up flush.

44. When dry, trim the edges to produce a neat rectangle and tape in place centrally on the lid.

45. Cut gently around this rectangle using the straightedge. Remove the piece and any tape. Then reinforce the cuts, using your scalpel while placing the straightedge on the outside of the rectangle.

Remove the waste by chisel or freehand routing just to the depth of the veneer—any deeper and you will have a sunken panel! Apply some 10 percent diluted pva, tape the piece in place and put under pressure. To achieve the needed pressure, you can either use long reach clamps or put it in the press. In either case remember that the reverse of this is your playing surface and must be carefully protected—and you won't need much pressure. When this is dry, scrape absolutely flush.

46. If you want to work a decorative profile around the edge of the lid, now is the time to do it. I decided to use a simple profile cutter here with a fixed guide. Whatever you choose to do, don't go to full depth on the very first pass. Proceed cautiously. Do one pass to remove the bulk and then one or two further passes, removing a minimum of material, to bring it to its full depth. With maple, keep the speed down to about one-half the normal maximum to avoid leaving scorch marks. Now apply whatever finish you applied to your playing surfaces.

Fitting the Hinges

47. I usually fit my hinges using the router/table set up to define the depth in the following way. Position the lid and base with the edges to be hinged together and with a sharp pencil mark exactly where you want your hinges to go—in this case, 1⅜" in from the ends seems about right. With a small square placed outside these lines, score them deeply with a scalpel—it is important that you cut to the full depth of the hinge at the front and back of each line to avoid any breaking away during routing.

Set the router up with a square cutter—the bigger the better, but size is not important as long as it is smaller than the length of the hinge—and adjust the height of the cut to be exactly one-half of the height of the hinge at the knuckle. Test this on scrap first.

Set a fence 1⅜" from the near side of the cutter and make a cut passing both ends of both box halves over it. Now make further passes with the fence set so that the far edge of the cutter is ¹⁄₃₂" less from the fence than the inner edge of your chosen hinges are from the ends of the box halves.

47

48

48. Open up these recesses with a wide chisel so that the hinges slot into place. Screw the hinges into place on the lid with all their screws, then attach this to the base with one screw per hinge—don't drill the other holes yet. If the lid and base line up exactly when you close the box, fine—drill all remaining holes dead center and fit the other screws. If not—which is much more likely—drill one further hole for each hinge so as to move the lid in the right direction to make any correction necessary.

49

Once you have a good fit, drill any remaining holes dead center and screw in place. Now give front, back, sides and inner edges a thorough sanding down to 320 grit, remove the hinges, and apply a coat of thinned sanding sealer. Allow to dry and sand, wire wool and wax the whole exterior, including inner edges, with a good quality clear furniture wax.

49. Now clean up your hinges and refit, replacing any damaged screws with pristine ones, and line up the slots.

50

Fitting the Catch

50. Stick a piece of masking tape along the middle of the front edge. Here I have fitted a simple flip-up type—you may choose whatever you wish. For this type of catch, which is often intended to be attached with pins, it is worth drilling out the holes, countersinking them, and fitting the catches on with small brass machine screws. See notes on "Cleaning Up Hardware," pages 20 and 21.

51

51. Choose your drill size carefully so that the screws cut their own firm thread.

52. Once you drill these holes for screws, you will find that you have a far more secure catch than one fitted with pins.

52

3 JEWELRY BOX

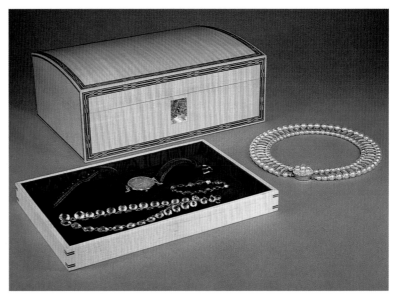

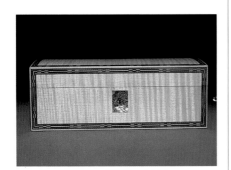

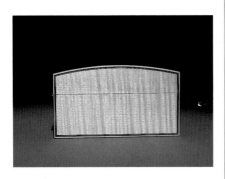

A curved lid always adds a bit of class to a box—this project shows you how to achieve a light, strong, and stable domed lid.

This is similar to Henry's Christening Box in that the sides are constructed from ⅜" birch ply with solid wood lipping where the lid meets the base and at the bottom. I used in this case plain maple, and the exterior veneer is a beautifully figured flamed maple.

I have jointed this box using miters—this is a good method as long as you have a way of cutting really reliable, clean miters. I have used a miter trimmer (the type used by picture framers) to do this. You could also form these by sawing using a miter saw and cleaning up afterwards with a disc sander, if necessary. The joints will be strengthened later with internal miter keys.

■ *Colored Lines* I used a blue and yellow line to go with a particularly beautiful piece of abalone I found for the escutcheon. It is well worth the effort making your own lines, and it is really not very difficult, but you can use any bought line or cross-banding.

This decoration has two basic elements: the outer lines and the decorative core. For the construction of the core a simple jig is necessary to apply longitudinal pressure to hold the elements together. When making decorative lines by stacking dyed veneers, it is essential that all the veneers you are using are of identical thickness or the heights of your stacks will not be the same. Even a tiny discrepancy can soon build up when you are using stacks of six or more veneers.

■ *Finish* If you intend to French polish this box, refer to the section on French polishing, pages 16 to 20, before you begin.

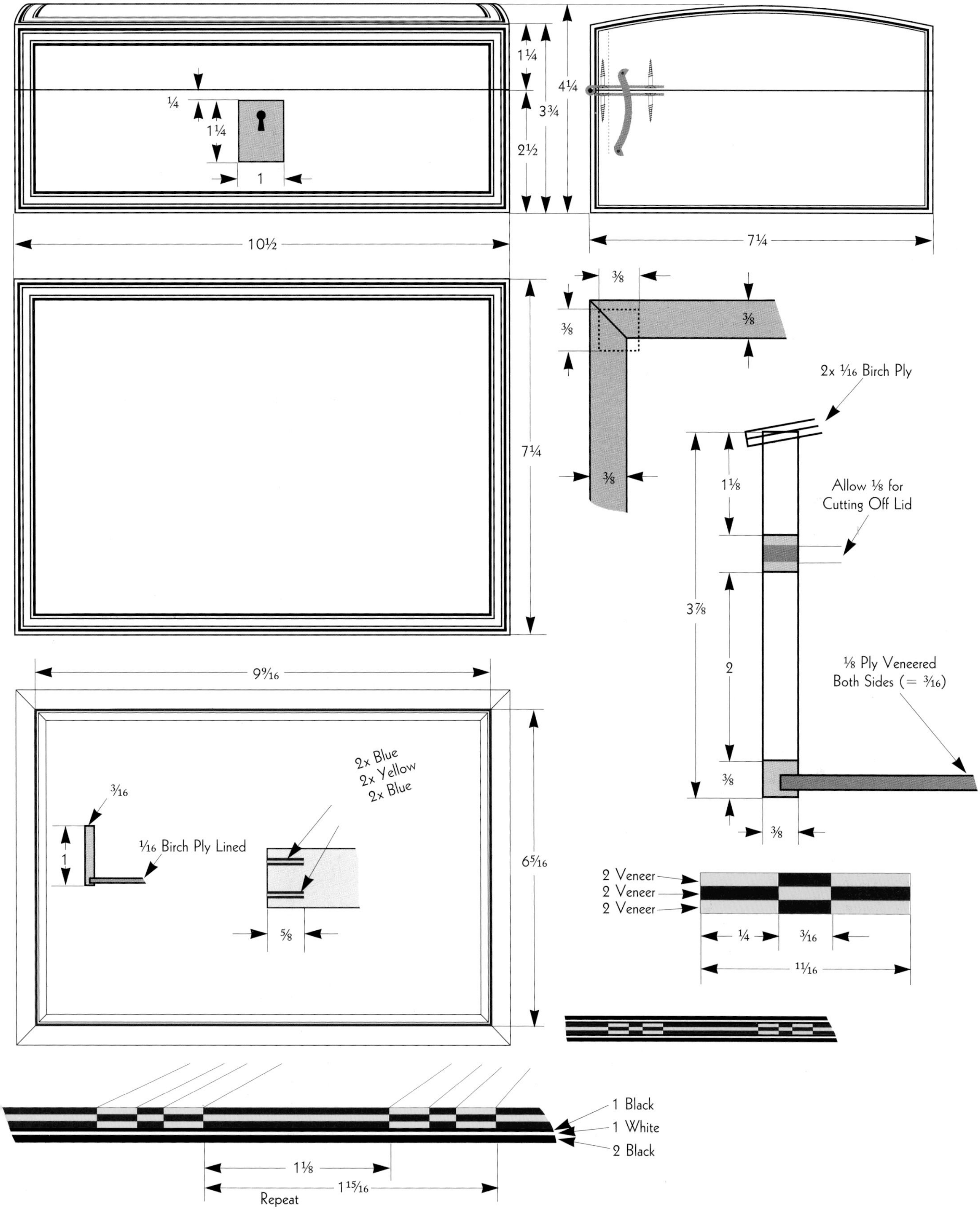
1¼
¼
1¼
1
2½
3¾
4¼
10½
7¼
⅜
⅜
⅜
⅜
7¼
2x 1⁄16 Birch Ply
1⅛
Allow ⅛ for Cutting Off Lid
3⅞
2
⅛ Ply Veneered Both Sides (= 3⁄16)
⅜
⅜
9⁹⁄16
3⁄16
2x Blue
2x Yellow
2x Blue
1⁄16 Birch Ply Lined
1
⅝
6⁵⁄16
2 Veneer
2 Veneer
2 Veneer
¼
3⁄16
11⁄16
1 Black
1 White
2 Black
1⅛
1¹⁵⁄16
Repeat

ELEMENT	MATERIAL	QTY	LENGTH	X x Y
MAIN BOX:				
FRONT & BACK	⅜" Birch Ply	2	10½" *	1⅛"
"	⅜" Birch Ply	2	"	2"
"	Maple	4	"	⅜" x ⅜"
SIDES	⅜" Birch Ply	2	7¼"	1⅛"
"	⅜" Birch Ply	2	"	2"
"	Maple	4	"	⅜" x ⅜"
LID	¹⁄₁₆" Birch Ply	2	11"	7¾"
BASE	⅛" Birch Ply	1	10½"	7¼"
TRAY				
FRONT & BACK	Figured (or Plain) Maple	2	9⁹⁄₁₆" *	1" x ³⁄₁₆"
SIDES	Figured (or Plain) Maple	2	⁵⁄₁₆" *	"
BASE	¹⁄₁₆" Birch Ply	1	9⁹⁄₁₆"	6⁵⁄₁₆" *

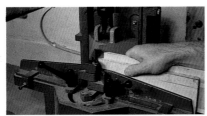

1

2

3

Preparing for Assembly

Prepare the pieces for the sides (see Project 1, the Diskette Box) to the dimensions in the plans and veneer a piece of ⅛" birch ply with plain maple on both sides for the base. Sand the base thoroughly, apply a coat of thinned SSS, allow to dry, and then apply a full strength coat. Set aside to dry.

1. Cut the miters as described above.

2. Make sure that you are cutting absolutely vertically. Tape together to check that the pieces are going together perfectly squarely and that they don't wobble (angles too sharp) or cause the outer corners to be open (angles too blunt).

3. When satisfied, make a template for the curve of the lid, as shown in the plan, and join the two end pieces together with double-sided (ds) tape, their outer faces facing out. Draw around the template onto one side, and cut out both pieces together using the band saw or a coping saw. Smooth the curve with the two pieces still united, preferably on a disc sander. This method will ensure that the edges are square and that you will get an identical shape at each end.

ELEMENT	MATERIAL	QTY	LENGTH	X x Y
VENEERS:				
FRONT & BACK	Figured Maple	2	11"	4¼"
SIDES	Figured Maple	2	7¾"	4¾"
LID	Figured Maple	1	11"	7¾"
BASE	Plain Maple	2	10½"	7¼"
VENEERS FOR COLORED LINES:				
	Black	3	13½"	4"
	White (Holly?)	1	13½"	4"
	Blue	4	12½"	2"
	Blue	2	3¾"	2"
	Yellow	2	12½"	2"
	Yellow	4	3¾"	2"
OTHER LINES:				
B/B/W/B	Bought or Homemade	-	11' approx.	-
	Boxwood Lines	-	7' approx.	⅛" square
PLUS:	Quadrant hinges, screws, lock, abalone and lining materials.			

4. Go over the base with 1200-grit wet and dry paper and 0000 wire wool to produce a nice, smooth surface. Take the pieces for the sides and cut the grooves to take the base using a ³⁄₁₆" straight cutter in the router. Along the mitered edges of the side pieces, cut short ⅛" grooves, ¼" deep, to take the ply miter keys. When making these cuts, use a stop to define the length of the cut as shown in the plan. You will need to make all of these cuts with the bottoms of the prepared pieces held securely against the fence due to the curve of the ends. Cut the miter keys from ⅛" ply, and glue one side of these in place in the grooves you have cut in the end pieces.

4

5. When the ply miter keys are dry, the side pieces are ready to be assembled. Remove any excess glue from around the miter keys and first assemble the box without any glue but with the base in place to check for fit.

5

6

7

8

9

10

11

Assembly

6. If satisfied, apply 10 percent diluted pva to the miters.

7. Tape up tightly and set aside to dry. With all this assembling and disassembling the tape can lose its stretch and it is best to use fresh tape for the final gluing up.

8. When the assembled box is dry reduce the top edge of the front and back down to the level of the ends by planing. Be careful that the angle you are planing at is a genuine continuation of the curve and work inwards from each end.

9. Cut the lid off using a ⅛" cutter and don't cut right through. You must measure this from the bottom of the box and leave about ⅟₁₆".

10. Cut through finally with a scalpel. The margin where you have cut off the lid will need to be cleaned up—do this with a piece of 180-grit garnet paper attached to the underside of a piece of scrap, working in a gentle grinding motion.

Making the Domed Lid

11. Now make the forms for making the lid (one inner and one outer, as shown in Steps 11 through 13—see also "Jigs & Aids," page 12). Mark around your template onto the end of a piece of ¾" mdf or similar, and cut out the concave shape, a little larger overall than the lid. Remove this material first by routing using a 1" round cutter. Then remove the ridges using a hollow plane. The interior form is easier as this can be shaped using any flat soled plane.

The final stages of the shaping of both forms are done with coarse abrasive paper (80- or 100-grit garnet) on curved blocks, using a circular grinding motion to remove any unevenesses. It is not necessary to make the interior form the full depth of your lid; in fact it is preferable to make it fairly shallow as this allows its use for a box that you may want to make later with a shallower lid. The height is made up in this case by using pieces of scrap and then card to make it really accurate. An alternative could be to cut out a few of the shapes on the band saw and glue these together on a piece of scrap to form the full length. You will then need to level the two halves carefully so they accurately represent your original template. In order to form the lid it is best to use a veneer press. A small veneer press is invaluable for this sort of work, and they are available occasionally from second hand or junk shops and well worth snapping up. If you don't have one you will need some rigid boards, some lengths of sturdy angle iron to spread the load evenly, and plenty of clamps big enough to take the depth of the whole assembly.

12. Place the inner form in the lid raised up with scrap so that its edges are absolutely flush with the frame all around. At this stage you can add some bits of card to the form if you detect any slight dips or discrepancies.

13. Cut two pieces of ¹⁄₁₆" birch ply a little over size with the grain of the face veneers running lengthwise on both pieces. Apply full-strength pva around the lid frame, put one piece of ply in place, then the carpet underlay, the ⅛" ply on top of that, and finally the top form. Place in the press or clamp up in between your rigid boards, etc.

14. When dry—after about ½ hour—remove from pressure and apply a coat of 10 percent diluted pva to the first layer of ply, put the second in place, and set up as before.

When this is dry, you will need to correct any slight distortion that may have occurred in the laminating process—even with a well fitting form in place a small amount of "dipping" can take place—a little judicious planing and/or scraping at each end will ensure that the lid is level and true—keep checking with a straightedge.

When satisfied, apply another layer of diluted pva and veneer the lid while the support is still in place, setting up as before.

As soon as you remove the lid from the press or clamp set-up give the newly veneered surface a thorough sanding and a coat of thinned shellac sanding sealer and then, when dry, another full strength coat. This is an important discipline whenever you are using any very light-colored veneer—it will protect the delicate, light color from getting dirty from the dust generated by subsequent operations. When dry, trim off excess ply and veneer from around the lid edges by bandsawing and plane flush with the sides.

15. The lid is veneered first because the laminating and veneering processes sometimes cause the front and back of the lid to splay out slightly. This is a serious problem if all other elements have already been veneered because the amount of correction available to you is severely limited by the thinness of the veneer. Check the fit of lid and base to see if there is any discrepancy and if necessary correct with a little cautious scraping and/or sanding with the three faces that you are not working on taped together.

When lid and base fit perfectly, proceed to veneer the rest of the exterior surfaces as set out in Project 1, the "Diskette Box." Note that you do not need to veneer the inner edges of the lid and box for this project. When you have veneered all faces, give all surfaces a coat of thinned sanding sealer and then another couple of coats of full-strength shellac sanding sealer for protection.

12

13

14

15

16

17

18

19

20

21

22

23

Making the Colored Banding

The outer layer, working inwards, is a double layer of black, then one each of white and black, and the core is made from laminated sandwiches of dyed veneers of various proportions. Prepare the outer layer in one piece, 13" x 4" (three black and one white), and when laminated, cut in two down its length to produce the two outer layers.

16. The inner core is a bit more involved: Prepare a sandwich (two blue, two yellow, two blue) 12" x 2" (this will also yield the triangles needed to provide the miter keys for the tray) and another, smaller one (two yellow, two blue, two yellow), 3¼" x 2".

17. Cut the prepared sandwiches into their required sizes using a small band saw and fence.

18. Trim the edges of all your prepared components so that they are square and smooth by planing as shown—note that the pieces are held in place by a fence with a little shoulder in it.

19. Tape one piece of your outer layer, double black out (down) on a rigid board, apply glue to a half of its length, and tape your prepared core elements in place on it in the desired combination, applying glue between the elements as you go.

20. Apply the tightening jig (made from mdf and steel studding, as shown) to close up the elements, place a piece of paper and a board to hold them down flat, place in the veneer press or apply a moderate amount of pressure with clamps onto the outer layer, and set aside. When dry, repeat with the other half of the elements. Plane the top surface of this assembly to ensure that all the elements are completely level and, when satisfied, apply the final outside layer.

21. Now plane both edges until you are producing complete, unbroken shavings and they are absolutely straight and square. Cut off a ¹⁄₁₆" sliver from each planed edge on a small bandsaw—see page 10 on making the most of small band saws. Replane each sawn edge and continue until you have enough lines for your project.

Fitting Decorative Lines & Squares

22. Tape lid and box together, and cut around with a purfling cutter (see "Jigs & Aids," page 13)—you must remove two different amounts of veneer as follows:

Lid and front: just less than the width of your decorative line plus the box square. Sides and back: just less than the width of the B/B/W/B plus the box square.

23. Reinforce all cuts to full veneer depth with a sharp scalpel and remove the veneer with a sharp chisel, scraping with the end if necessary to arrive at a smooth surface.

24. Fit the wide decorative lines, first starting with the ends of the lid, mitering the pieces as you go.

24

25. Fit the BB/W/B lines (as explained in Project 1, the Diskette Box, pages 29 to 33), but since the lid and base are already separate pieces all the scalpel/purfling cuts need to be made with the box taped together. Also, working with a curved shaped top such as this makes the use of the router difficult, but you could use it for the initial cuts along the bottom edges and up the sides if you want—I usually stick to doing the whole lot by hand. If you are using figured maple, as I have done here, or any other delicate veneer, it is advisable to do this job following the precautions set out in Project 1. You should be all right when cutting across the grain but tiny segments of the delicate waves that are the hallmark of fiddle back maple tend to fall off when you are cutting with the grain.

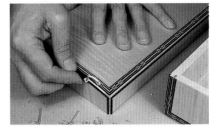

25

Fitting Lock & Escutcheon

26. Place the lock upside down centrally on the front edge of the box with its back plate flush with the inside of the box and mark around it. Reinforce these lines with the scalpel, and remove the maple so that the top of the lock fits into the recess flush.

26

27. Clamp the box to the bench on its front and cut with a wide flat chisel until the back plate of the lock fits flush in this recess.

28. Similarly remove the waste necessary to accommodate the works of the lock and allow it to fit the right way round. Drill for the keyhole and file until the key fits and can work the lock. Now fit the quadrant hinges (exactly the same way as in Project 1, the Diskette Box, pages 33 and 34).

27

29. With the hinges fitted so that the lid and box match perfectly, tape the lock top plate in place, as shown. Then close the lid on it. The registering lugs on the top plate will then show exactly where to locate this in the front edge of the lid. Mark around the plate, chisel out so that it is flush, and screw in position. Hold the escutcheon in place, cut around it, and remove the veneer from this section. You may need to go a little deeper than just the thickness of the veneer—it is always best that mother-of-pearl and abalone are inlaid as flush as possible because they are very hard and difficult to bring down flush to their surroundings. When fitted and scraped flush as necessary (don't sand yet), drill and file through to your original keyhole, and apply another coat of full-strength SSS to the front.

28

29

30

31

32

33

34

35

30. Sand the front completely level and apply a final coat of SSS (or 50/50 FP/SSS). Give all exterior surfaces a thorough sanding and the box is now ready for polishing (see the section on French polishing, pages 16 to 20).

Making the Tray

The tray is a simple, plain tray with no divider—you could add one. I have used simple miters strengthened with colored miter keys. The base is fitted into grooves along the inside bottom edges.

31. Measure the internal dimensions of your box and subtract ³⁄₁₆" from each to give you the dimensions for your tray. Mark these exact values on your pieces using a sharp scriber and a small square, and cut them slightly over length. Saw/chop/sand the miters and work the grooves around the inner bottom edges for the base—I have used ¹⁄₁₆" birch ply for lightness.

32. Cut the base to size, assemble with masking tape to check for fit, and repeat with glue if satisfied. I use slightly watered-down pva for the miters to avoid glue building up in the joints, stopping them from closing up properly.

33. When dry sand top and bottom flush using a sanding stick—see "Useful Jigs & Aids," pages 12 to 13.

If you didn't make your own line for this project (or you haven't any of the elements left over) laminate a sandwich of dyed veneers to match those in the decorative line you used —preferably exactly the format of the longer section of the core of the line, in this case two blue, two yellow, two blue. You will not need very much: a single lamination 1" x 2½" with the grain of all pieces running along its length. Cut in two along its length it will yield eight right-angle triangles ¾" x ½" x ¼" with the grain running along the long edge— the hypotenuse. Plane the edges of each strip absolutely straight and square and cut into triangles by cutting across the strips at 45°. The planed edge will be the inner face.

34. Make the cuts for the keys using your miter key cutting jig and a ⅛" square cutter on the router. If you haven't made this jig already, now may be the time (see "Useful Jigs & Aids," page 13). You can mark these out by hand, cutting out using a fine dovetail saw and cleaning up with a sharp chisel, if you go very carefully, but this is quite difficult. The jig, provided it is truly vertical, is easy to use and accurate.

35. Apply some full-strength pva to your cuts and insert the triangles, ensuring that the grain runs across the corners and the planed faces go inwards.

36. When dry, trim off the excess by careful chiseling, working away from the corners as shown. Sand only after you have applied another coat of thinned sanding sealer and allowed it to dry. When all the corners are completely flush, apply a coat of full-strength sanding sealer and set aside to dry thoroughly. For a lovely, matte, silky feel, smooth gently with 1200-grit wet and dry paper and 0000 wire wool and wax with a good quality clear furniture wax.

If you want to fit a divider across the halfway mark, then do this with a bit of the same wood cut to length and exactly fitted by trimming it precisely on the disc sander. Glue the divider in place, and strengthen with brass pins tapped in from outside (drill slightly undersized pilot holes first). Snip off the heads and smooth before the final finishing operations.

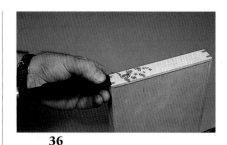

36

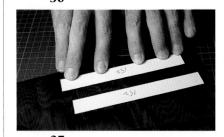

37

Lining

I usually line jewelry boxes using a combination of silk moiré and cotton velvet formed on card. I use the moiré for the vertical faces and the velvet for the horizontal surfaces in the bottoms of trays and in the main box and lid. Covering one side of a sheet of thin card with ds (double-sided) tape on one side is a useful preparation for any lining operation. The various sizes of card that you need can then be cut from it ready to be used.

38

37. Cut pieces of prepared card slightly overlength for the back and front of your tray. Remove the backing from the ds tape and place it sticky side down onto the reverse side of a piece of moiré as shown. Cut around them flush with the card along the bottoms and both ends but leaving spare material along the top edges. Fold the top edges over and secure with another piece of ds tape. Trim exactly to length, glue in place in the tray with latex adhesive and repeat for the ends. Measure the internal dimensions of the tray with these pieces in place and cut another piece of the card slightly undersize. Cover this with velvet in the same way but leaving spare material all the way around.

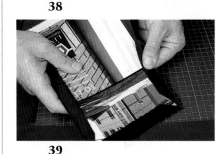

39

38. Attach ds tape around the edges of the reverse side, and cut the corners away as shown.

40

39. With the corners cut away, fold over the velvet all around the edges of the card.

40. Push the card lining assembly into the bottom of the tray.

41. Repeat for the whole interior of the main box in exactly the same way, except that you will need to incorporate a step of hardboard or similar into the side pieces of the main box to support the tray.

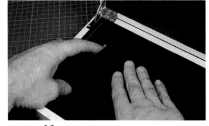

41

4 HENRY'S CHRISTENING BOX

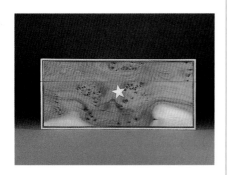

This box was made to contain items given to the son of a friend of mine at his christening. Although yew can be wild and difficult to use, I chose it for this box because it is a beautiful, rich, elegant veneer and well worth the extra effort necessary to use it properly. It tends to be very crinkly in its natural state, particularly when it is highly figured, and will usually need to be flattened before it can be used. This is done by dampening it and pressing it between rigid boards, using paper to absorb the moisture. It can also be very dry and crumbly, making inlaying work difficult and painstaking.

The sides are constructed incorporating cherry lipping for the inner edges and bottom, veneered on both sides and jointed using a simple rabbet cut in the ends of the pieces for front and back. This affords a large glue area and produces a strong joint.

■ **Decoration** I have kept the decoration to a minimum to allow the beauty of the yew to shine. The simple mother-of-pearl motifs were inspired by a design on the original christening card, and add a bit of extra interest. They are, however, difficult to inlay really neatly and some practice on a piece of scrap is a good idea.

You might like to make a tray for this to make the most of the height. Yew can be a difficult wood to use in the solid state, particularly if the dimensions you require are long and/or thin—cherry, which I have used here to lip the inner edges and base, is a good alternative which blends well and works easily.

■ **Finish** If you intend to French polish this box refer to the section on French polishing, pages 16 to 20, before you begin.

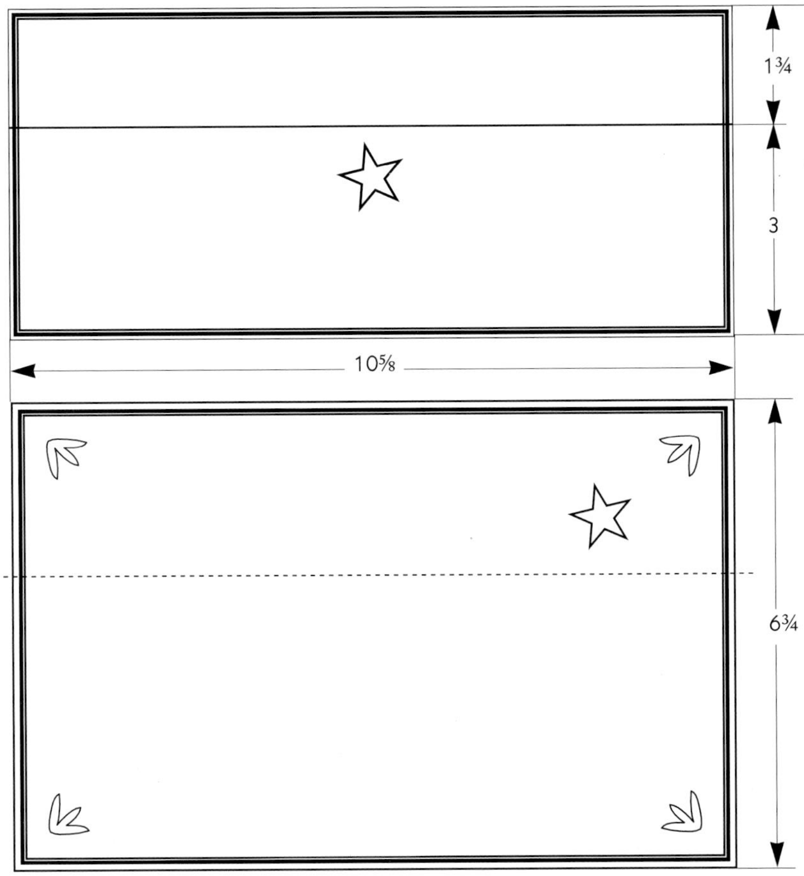
1¾
4¾
3
10⅝
6¾

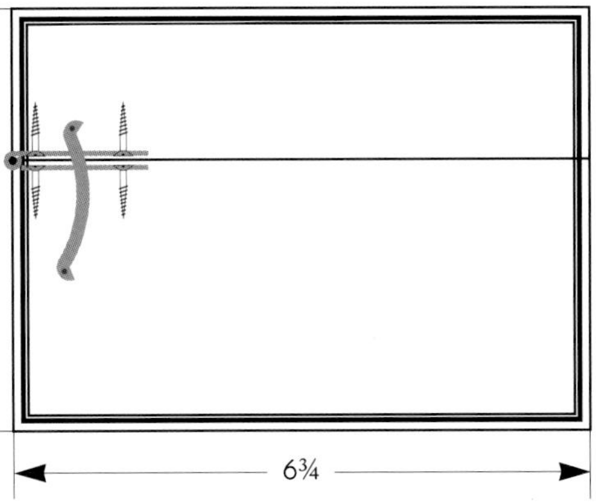
6¾

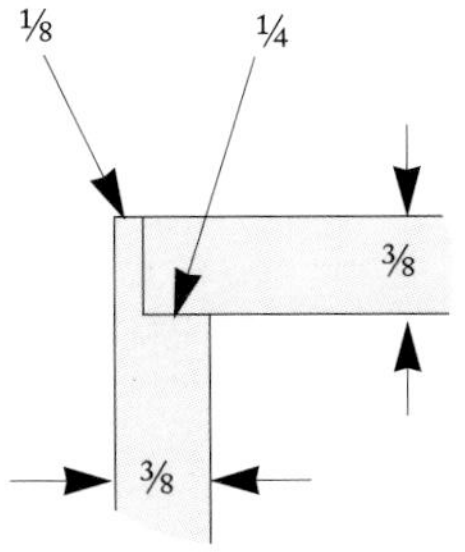
⅛
¼
⅜
⅜

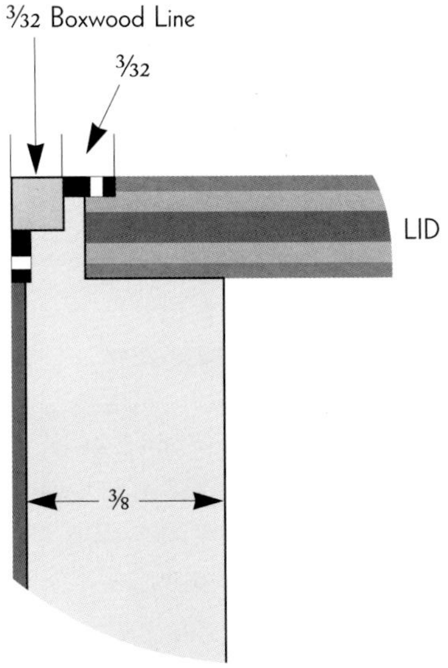
3/32 Boxwood Line
3/32
LID
⅜

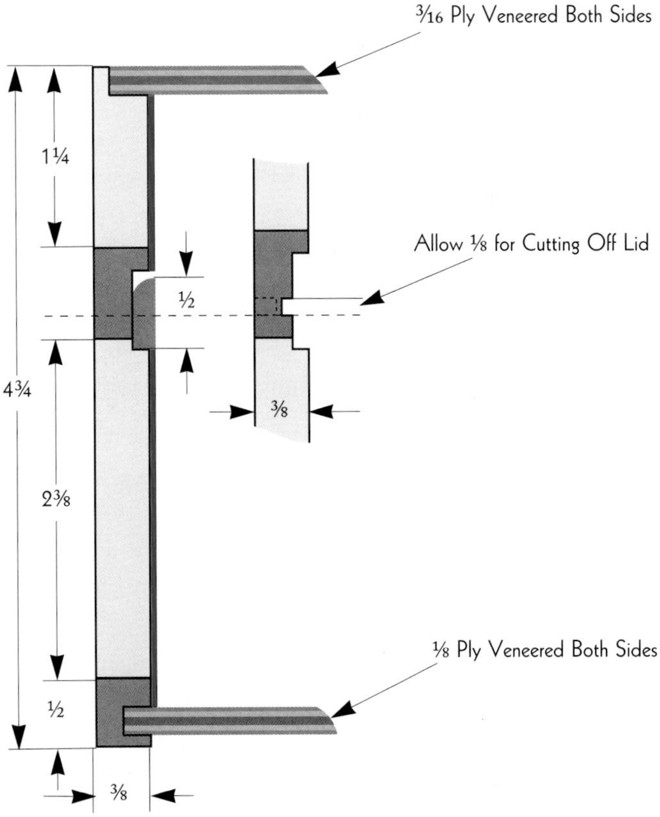
3/16 Ply Veneered Both Sides
1¼
½
Allow ⅛ for Cutting Off Lid
4¾
⅜
2⅜
⅛ Ply Veneered Both Sides
½
⅜

ELEMENT	MATERIAL	QTY	LENGTH	X x Y
FRONT & BACK	⅜" Birch Ply	2	10⅝" *	1¼"
"	⅜" Birch Ply	2	10⅝"	2⅜"
"	Cherry	2	10⅝"	⅜" x ⅜"
"	Cherry	2	10⅝"	⅜" x ½"
SIDES	⅜" Birch Ply	2	6½"	1¼"
"	⅜" Birch Ply	2	6½"	2⅜"
"	Cherry	2	6½"	⅜" x ⅜"
"	Cherry	2	6½"	⅜" x ½"
LID	3⁄16" Birch Ply	1	10⅝"	6¾"
BASE	⅛" Birch Ply	1	10⅝"	6¾"
LIPPING	Cherry	1	10⅝"	½" x 3⁄16"

VENEERS

FRONT & BACK	Figured Yew (Good)	2	10⅞"	5¼"
"	Figured Yew (Balance)	2	10⅞"	5¼"
SIDES	Figured Yew (Good)	2	7¼"	5¼"
"	Figured Yew (Balance)	2	7¼"	5¼"
LID	Figured Yew (Good)	1	10⅞"	7¼"
"	Figured Yew (Balance)	1	10⅞"	7¼"

OTHER LINES:

B/B/W/B	Bought or Homemade	-	11' approx	-
	Boxwood Lines	-	7' approx.	⅛" square

PLUS: Quadrant hinges, screws and lining materials.

1

2

Preparing the Front, Back & Sides

The pieces for the sides of the box must first be constructed. I have used ⅜" birch plywood with pieces of cherry sandwiched in between. Each side consists of two pieces of ply and two pieces of cherry, as shown in the plan. This ensures that the final piece appears to be made from solid cherry and no nasty striped bits of ply show.

Cut the pieces of ply just oversize—by about ¼"—in each dimension and plane the long edges absolutely square and true. Now cut the cherry to size. This is best done so that you produce one piece, long enough to allow for one long and one short side, but wide enough to produce four pieces ¹⁄₁₆" thicker than the ply. Cut this into strips on the band saw to produce pieces of the required width and then cut slightly over length.

1. Glue the cherry to the ply—the glue is best applied in one long blob along the edge, and then spread evenly by rubbing the cherry against it.

2. Tape the pieces firmly in place with masking tape, checking that you are allowing a small overlap on both sides of the piece of ply for planing flush later.

3. When the pieces are dry, remove the tape and plane the cherry flush on one side only. You can do this by setting the plane so that it is quite fine and by also tilting the blade very slightly so that the plane is cutting at the left hand side of a pass, but not quite at the right hand side. This arrangement reduces the risk of the right hand side digging in and causing a gash that would then need to be filled. It also allows you to adjust the depth of cut at will—removing a thicker shaving initially and a thinner one later—simply by moving the plane slightly to the left or right (reverse all the rights for lefts if you are left-handed!).

4. Plane the cherry edge of each piece you have prepared so that it is square.

5. Butt-joint the pairs together, clamped onto a rigid board as shown with the planed faces down, to produce the pieces for each of the four sides.

6. When these completed pieces are dry, plane the un-planed sides flush, and true up the planed sides if necessary.

7. Plane these pieces exactly to the required dimensions—check particularly that opposing pairs of pieces are identical in length.

8. They are now ready to be veneered.

3

4

5

6

7

8

9

10

11

12

13

14

Preparing the Veneer for Front, Back & Sides

9. Select your veneer carefully, to produce the effect you need, and cut out. Here I have chosen some nice pieces of figured yew and some not-so-nice pieces of yew for the reverse—interior—sides of the pieces. The veneer for the sides, front, and back were available in one piece—I had the required width—but in order to get the correct dimensions for the lid I needed to join two pieces. This is always a golden opportunity to use any nice decorative features in the veneer to produce a good mirror or "book-matched" effect. In order to achieve this you must have several—or at least two—consecutive leaves of veneer cut from the same piece. This needs to be joined carefully and I will deal with this later.

10. The best way to flatten crinkly veneer ready for use is to place a piece of your selected veneer on something waterproof and completely flat—a piece of kitchen work surface or Formica is ideal—and then paint some water onto both sides of the veneer, covering it all.

11. Then soak up as much of the excess water as you can using tissue, and place the veneer on three or four sheets of paper on another piece of the kitchen work surface, placing another three or four pieces of paper on top. Place the first board on top and put in a veneer press (alternatively, clamp up firmly using clamps and pieces of angle iron to spread the pressure). Leave this for a couple of hours and then replace the paper to soak up the rest of the moisture, and replace under pressure.

Don't be tempted to try to use the veneer before it is absolutely dry, otherwise it will shrink after it has been applied and will eventually cause unsightly cracks to open up on the surface of your finished piece.

Veneering the Pieces

12. Tape two pieces of your flattened veneer for the outside onto a flat board with a piece of paper underneath. Apply an even coat of 10 percent diluted pva with a 1" brush reserved for this purpose.

13. Place the pieces to be veneered in position and apply more glue. Place the veneer for the inside on this, followed by another piece of paper, some carpet underlay, and another flat board, and place in the veneer press. As with the flattening process, you will probably be able to do this at least two pieces at a time depending on the size of your press or clamp set up.

14. When these pieces are dry and sound—probably after about an hour—remove them from the pressure and trim any excess veneer from around all edges using a sharp scalpel or craft knife. These pieces are now ready to be jointed and have the various necessary grooves cut in them.

Cutting the Joints

Set the router up with a cutter larger than ½" to cut to about three-quarters of the required finished depth and width. With the first piece held firmly in a "T" bar (see "Jigs & Aids," page 13), slowly and gently move the back corner of the piece onto the cutter—this trims the end of the cut first without the risk of the grain breaking away when the cutter exits at the end of the cut.

15

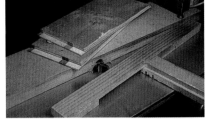

16

15. When you have done the cuts to the ¾ dimensions for the two pieces, adjust the cutter to cut the full depth of the rabbet and complete the cuts.

16. You should now have a cleanly cut rabbet at each end of each of the pieces for front and back which should neatly accommodate the full thickness of the sides.

17

Grooves & Rabbets

17. Now cut the various grooves and rabbets along these pieces to take the lid, base, and liner and to form one half of the lid cut-off groove as indicated in the plan. These can be worked in any order, except that the wide groove for the liner should be cut before the lid cut-off groove to avoid the possibility of the grain breaking away along its inner edges when the wider groove is cut. Cut the lid cut-off groove with the base against the fence (the tops of the box will have been planed flush by the time you cut off the lid) and make a reference cut on a piece of scrap so that you can accurately set up the router later for cutting the other half.

18

18. Note that the lipping groove must stop before the front ends of the side pieces—make a mark on the fence to ensure this. Also note that there is no lipping along the back of the box.

19

19. Veneer a piece of ⅛" birch ply for the base with some straight grain cherry. Veneer this, cut exactly to size, apply some shellac sanding sealer, and smooth when dry. You will need to have this, but not the lid, ready in order to glue the box together.

20. Two details still need to be dealt with before the box is ready to be glued up. First, the thin strip of veneer along the bottom, inner edge of each piece needs to be removed. This is best done carefully paring away using a sharp chisel as shown.

20

21

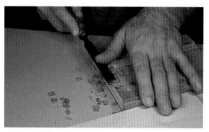

22

23

24

25

26

21. Then the veneer along the inner face of the two side pieces which will be glued as part of the joint must also be removed.

22. Mark lines using a scalpel with the pieces for front/back in place, reinforce using a scalpel and straightedge and remove. Now these pieces are ready to be glued up.

Gluing up the Box

23. You should allow for a bit of time and effort to go into the planning at this stage. You need to be prepared so that you are ready to exert the pressure in exactly the right places, without distorting the box and without having to resort to taking complex and time-consuming emergency measures while the glue is rapidly hardening! A few nice, sliding-head clamps make life a great deal easier, but there are usually ways around not having them.

Here I have used two medium-sized sliding-head clamps and four others, but what makes this operation a lot easier and safer is clamping the box down on its front onto a completely flat work-surface as shown.

24. It is important to prepare a sturdy mdf piece, to fit across the back of the box to help spread the pressure evenly, and another two pieces for each end. I have used some slightly concave pieces at each end of this piece to enable me to use one clamp for each end. The pieces for the ends must just fit in between the slightly protruding ends of the front and back so as to be exerting pressure on the actual joint. It is very important that the pressure is in the right places to make the joints good and tight.

Do a dry run, check that all is working as it should.

25. When satisfied that all is going to run smoothly, apply glue, assemble and apply clamps as practiced during your dry run. Check for squareness—this should not be a problem, however, as your piece for the base should have been cut completely square and will fit snugly enough into place to keep the assembly square.

If you do have any squareness problems, it is worth having a spare sliding-head clamp or two available to do a bit of last-minute minor diagonal clamping. Use your commonsense abilities to determine which way the pressure needs to be applied. Release a little of the pressure to the other clamps first, otherwise you will end up having to apply huge amounts of pressure to effect any change. Basically, it is best not to exert too much pressure all around—in any case, it should not be necessary if the joints are well cut and the base is the correct size.

Veneering the Lid

Make up a piece of SuperPly (see Project 2, the Backgammon Board, pages 36 and 38) a little oversized for the lid and veneer it with the prepared joined and flattened pieces you have selected.

26. If you are book-matching as I have done here, take your two selected pieces of veneer, before flattening, and decide roughly where you want to cut them to produce the best effect.

27. Cut these with a scalpel and straightedge, allowing a little extra for recutting the join after flattening. When the pieces are completely flat and dry, cut the joint again, remembering to reverse the cut for the second piece so that any error will be canceled out. You may need to cut this three or four times to get a really clean join. The cleanest cut will be achieved by removing the smallest possible amount of material with the sharpest possible blade. Undercutting slightly also helps. With particularly tricky veneers you may find it necessary to re-dampen and flatten the veneer if it starts to distort slightly. It is not necessary to go through the whole flattening procedure again; a fine mist with a plant mister and a short period under pressure with a couple of sheets of paper will often suffice. As before, though, it is necessary that the veneer is completely dry before it is actually veneered to anything.

28. When you have achieved a good join, tape one piece down on a flat board with a piece of masking tape underneath where the join will be and run a small amount of glue along the edge of the other piece and tape that in position.

29. Run the curved end of a small metal ruler along the join to flatten it. A few masking tape "stitches" along the join will help to hold it together. Put a piece of paper over this, and another flat board, and put under a small amount of pressure. This will not take long to dry, perhaps half an hour, after which time remove it from the pressure, remove tape, etc., and place between weighted boards until you are ready to use it, which should be soon.

30. Now veneer your prepared piece to the SuperPly for the lid: tape your book-matched piece face down onto a setting up board with paper underneath, apply 10 percent diluted pva, and place the SuperPly on it.

31. Apply more glue, place the veneer for the inside on this, then another piece of paper, the carpet underlay and the second board. Place in the press for an hour or so.

32. When dry, remove it from the press, and trim excess veneer from its edges.

27

28

29

30

31

32

33

34

35

36

37

38

Cutting the Lid to Size

33. Unclamp your box and give it a good look over to see how everything went. Hopefully all will have gone well. Remove any excess glue from the joints at the corners of the lid rabbet to allow it to sit absolutely flush and level, and measure the exact dimensions for the lid.

Cut the lid exactly to size—it should be a neat, push fit and it should sit fractionally below the top of the sides of the box which will be planed flush later.

If you get the lid stuck in its rabbet, turn the box upside down and tap one end gently on the bench—this should dislodge it. If this doesn't work, try a bit harder, and if you still can't remove it, you shouldn't have pushed it into place in the first place! As you are going to be covering up the join between the lid and the box with decoration anyway, in an emergency like this you can gouge away with a small chisel until the lid pops out. However, try not to damage the lid too much—there is not much space to spare on the inside of the join.

Gluing on the Lid

34. When satisfied, apply glue around the rabbet, push the lid into place and clamp gently.

35. The pieces that you have prepared for clamping the sides of the box should be just right for the task of holding the lid in place, as shown.

36. When the assembly is dry, remove the clamps and trim down the tops of the sides of the box so that the top is completely flush. This is best done first using a plane set up as it was for planing the cherry lipping flush—that is, with a very slight misalignment of the blade and sole to prevent the right hand corner of the blade from digging in.

37. When I have managed to trim the top down so that it is very nearly flush, I will usually then change to a cabinet scraper to finish the job—I find that using a scraper in one hand and pulling it toward me while I am holding the box firm with the other is a good way of doing this.

38. When you have worked with both the plane and the cabinet scraper to get the top completely level, give the whole surface of the lid a good scrape. As you scrape the surface at this stage, be careful not to tear the grain at all. Then sand with 180-grit, followed by 240-grit garnet paper.

Smoothing up the Sides

39. Now remove any overlap at the joints on the sides of the box by planing as before. A variation to the slightly offset plane iron method is to use a wide chisel with a piece of masking tape stuck around one corner to prevent it cutting on that side.

40. Finish completely flush by then scraping and sanding.

41. Your basic, veneered box is now ready to be prepared for decoration and for cutting off the lid.

39

40

Dealing with Problem Veneers

The method I have set out below for cutting the veneer in preparation for applying the decorative lines is necessary particularly when you are working with very dry, crumbly, and unforgiving veneers—such as, in this case, yew. The problem is that the thickness of the scalpel blade tends to compress the veneer on either side of the cut. With moist, springy, resilient veneers, this is fine because the wood merely springs back into place when you have made the cut, leaving you with a perfectly clean edge.

On problem veneers, however, the edges tend just to crumble. Sometimes—but only sometimes—the router set at high speed will do the cut back to the required line perfectly cleanly. Unfortunately, it is impossible to tell whether this will work until you have actually done it, by which time it is too late! So I recommend sticking with the above method, and doing the cutting in the same way every time.

41

42

Preparing to Apply the Decoration

First cut away the veneer from all round all of the edges. Do this in a strict order:

42. Mark both ends of each cut on all five faces using a purfling cutter (see "Useful Jigs & Aids," page 13, for a brief description and picture of my homemade purfling cutter).

43. Cut the lines full length, gently, using a straightedge and a sharp scalpel—half depth only.

44. Set the router to remove waste to within ¹⁄₆₄" of the scalpel line. Cut your original scalpel line to full depth all of the way around, removing the waste with the scalpel held flat, as shown. Then cut another, completely clean scalpel line, removing the tiniest possible amount of material to bring the amount removed to the required width.

43

44

45

46

47

48

49

50

45. This method is the safest and you should now have the box prepared with ultra-sharp edges cut all round.

46. Now cut the rabbets along all corners, slightly undersize, to take the boxwood squares.

Before Applying the Decoration

It may seem that a logical extension of doing this amount of work before cutting off the lid would be to actually apply the decoration first as well. There are two problems with this. First, the vertical pieces of boxwood square that you need to fit at each vertical corner have complex double miters at each end which are hard enough to get right one end at a time—getting both ends of a piece exactly right would be well nigh impossible. It is much easier if separate pieces for lid and base are allowed to bleed over the lid/base margin for later trimming—you only have to get one end right at a time. Second, even if you were able to do this job satisfactorily you would run the risk of splitting away some of the boxwood when you finally cut off the lid. Now is the time to cut off the lid.

Cutting Off the Lid

47. This should be straightforward as long as you made a reference cut when you cut the first half of the groove. Carefully set up the router fence to this value and cut at a depth such that you do not cut right through. There should be a remaining fraction left to be separated carefully by hand. The fraction remaining should be about about 1/64".

48. You should take time to remove this last 1/64" very carefully using your scalpel.

49. When the box is parted, clean up the inner edges of the base and lid with careful chiseling.

50. Sand smooth using a blind-ended sanding board—see the description in the section "Useful Jigs & Aids," page 13.

Making up the Decorative Lines

Now make up your BB/W/B lines.

These are produced simply by laminating black dyed veneer with something white and plain (holly, horse chestnut) into a sandwich. The assembled stack of veneers needs to be long enough for the longest line you need and wide enough to yield the number of pieces that you will need.

51. When you have prepared this sandwich, plane both edges straight and square.

52. Cut strips from it on a carefully set up small band saw—see the discussion on small band saws on page 10. The smooth, planed face is the one that gets glued down.

51

Gluing the Lines in Place

Now the BB/W/B lines are glued in place, preferably in the following order:

> The long horizontal pieces along the top and bottom edges on all four faces.
>
> All the vertical pieces that culminate at the margin between lid and base.
>
> The pieces around the lid, long then short.

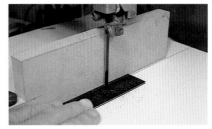

52

53. Apply a small amount of glue, spread out to the edges with a small stick, and fix the first pieces in place with masking tape.

Leave the cutting of the miters at the ends of these first pieces until they are all glued into place. I always start with a long side, that way the last bit that I fit is a short one. The last piece is always a little harder than the others, so is a bit more likely to have problems. This way I have a short piece as the last to work on, and, since it is the most likely to go wrong, I am protecting myself so that I waste the least amount possible.

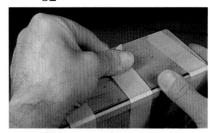

53

54. Mark the width of the vertical pieces by holding them in place, overlapping the pieces you have already glued into place and making a small cut with the scalpel.

54

55. Now mark the inside end of the miter and cut using a small, sharp chisel held vertically.

56. Cut the miter on the vertical piece to match. This can be done by eye using a small metal rule and the scalpel—if it doesn't quite match, it can always be slightly adjusted.

55

These cuts should ideally be completely vertical but it helps to undercut them very slightly. How much depends on how much thicker your lines are than the amount of material your router removed—preferably only the thickness of the veneer. If they are thicker by quite a lot, then too much undercutting will cause the two sides of the miter not to meet when the lines are brought down to the level of the veneer later. The ends of the lines can be thinned down a bit before doing the mitering, if you think this may be a problem.

56

57

58

59

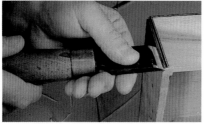

60

61

62

57. Once you have completed all the pieces on all four sides of the box, fit the pieces for the lid. The vertical pieces should overlap the lid/base margin by a small amount to allow for trimming flush before fitting the boxwood squares.

58. Trim these flush now by cutting with a scalpel and carefully sanding with a fine sanding stick.

59. Now trim back the rabbets previously cut out for the boxwood squares on the router so that they will go in absolutely flush to the edges of the BB/W/B lines. Do this with the scalpel, carefully running the non-cutting side of the blade along the edge of the BB/W/B lines, using them as a fence.

60. Undercut slightly and use a wide chisel, as shown.

61. When you have removed all the necessary waste and a piece of the boxwood square fits snugly against all the lines start to fit the squares in the following order: all long horizontal squares, top and bottom, all short horizontal, top and bottom, all vertical.

62. First cut a piece of the square a little overlong for one of the long sides, along the bottom of the front for example. Using a 45-degree block and a sharp chisel, cut a 45-degree angle at one end—my habit is to work from left to right doing this of job. Twist the piece through 90 degrees and make an identical cut, forming a neat double miter.

63. Put this in position and mark, either with a sharp pencil or the scalpel, where the miter at the other end needs to be. Cut this in the same way, possibly being a touch conservative—it can always be trimmed a fraction more—and again twist and cut to produce the double miter. If you do cut a piece a little short, you can always lengthen it. It's true—if you plane along the inside of the piece you will effectively increase the distance between the inside corners of the two miters. You will of course be reducing the thickness of the piece slightly, but you should have a little to play with.

When you have fitted the pieces on the top and bottom of the front and back, fit the shorter connecting pieces. Do this in exactly the same way as with the pieces already fitted, but you may need to adjust the angle of the ends where they meet the other pieces. Do this by either tipping the handle of the chisel forward to blunt the angle, or draw the miter block a little back from where you are making the cut to sharpen the angle.

At each top and bottom corner you should be forming a neat reverse shape to receive the vertical pieces with their double miters worked on the ends.

64. To fit the vertical lines, cut the double miters as before, but you will normally need to do a fair amount of messing about getting both sides of the joint to match properly. It helps to trim the boxwood back to almost the level of the surrounding veneer—this allows you get a better idea of how the finished joint will look. Also clean any glue from these corners. It is best to work the top, front corners last; these are most important and most likely to succeed if you have already had the practice of doing the other ones first!

65. When you have fitted all eight of these vertical pieces the protruding ends need to be trimmed flush to the lid/base margin. Do this using a piercing saw or a fine hacksaw, working inwards from the corners and then sanding gently with a leveling stick.

66. All lines and squares are now ready to be brought down to veneer level to give a completely flush finish. These can either be planed down (offset the iron slightly as before) or carefully pared away with a chisel.

67. In either case, do the final work with a sharp cabinet scraper. It helps to tape the box together along front back and sides—this allows you to work on the box as a single piece.

68. When you have arrived at a smooth, level surface all round and given all faces a good sanding, first 180 grit, then 240 grit, you are ready to fit the mother-of pearl decoration to the lid.

Cutting in the Mother-of-Pearl Details

Draw out your shapes carefully on masking tape stuck to your chosen pieces of mother-of-pearl. Make sure they are well defined. The best way to cut up mother-of-pearl is with a good quality fret saw machine, but I have used a piercing saw.

Using the Piercing Saw

Use a sharp blade—this is obvious, but I know from my own experience that one tends to go on just that little bit too long with a dull one. This means that you are having to use more force to achieve a reasonable rate of cut, which means you have to hold the piece down more firmly, the cut is more difficult to direct accurately and you are more likely to break the blade. Fit the blade so that it cuts on the down stroke; only apply pressure on the down stroke.

It can be easier to clamp down the piece you are cutting, but the more complicated the shape, the more it makes sense to hold it in place just by hand pressure because you will frequently need to adjust the orientation of the piece.

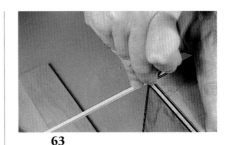

63

64

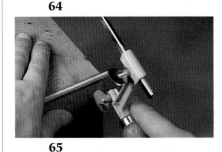

65

66

67

68

69

70

71

72

73

74

69. I used a good old-fashioned piercing saw, holding the piece firmly over a "V" cut out in a piece of mdf. Cut just outside the lines, following the shape as closely as you can, particularly on the inner edges, which you will not be able to get at to smooth using the disc sander.

When you have cut out the basic shapes as accurately as you can, these need to be carefully taken back exactly to the lines to give the shapes you require. You will be able to reach the external surfaces of the leaf shapes using the disc sander—use a fine disc and hold the piece securely on the table, adjusted so that it is at 90 degrees to the disc and as close to it as you can get it. To smooth the interior surfaces you will need some fine garnet paper, a few good needle files, especially a couple with one or more edges which do not cut but will act to hold the file in position while you are smoothing a different edge, and some patience.

70. Lay out the positions of the various pieces carefully on the lid using masking tape to mark their positions and proceed as follows: Hold a piece firmly in position and mark gently around it using the point of a fresh scalpel blade or craft knife. Don't attempt to cut to the full depth of the veneer at this stage. This can be a bit of an effort of contortion as you will need to keep swapping hands, continuing to hold the piece firmly in position while you rotate the lid in order to get yourself into the right positions to make all the necessary marks. If the piece does move you will have to re-position it as exactly as you can and carry on; this is not normally too serious but it is best to avoid it if you can. Once you have marked around the whole shape, remove the piece.

71. Now, still using the scalpel, make some cuts from the center of the area to be cut out to the edges, removing a thin sliver of veneer just the depth of your shallow marking cuts. Now the cuts can be deepened without fear of the veneer crumbling along the all important outer edge of the cut out. Remove the rest of the waste. I suggest that you cut down to take virtually the full thickness of your mother-of-pearl—this is likely to be about ¹⁄₁₆" and certainly no less than ¹⁄₃₂". Be careful when you are testing the piece for fit that you don't get it wedged in place. When you are satisfied with the fit, apply a little glue, and clamp a block over this to push it in flush. Repeat for the other three leaf details and the two stars.

72. When these are dry, bring them down flush to the surrounding veneer. As I have mentioned, this is not easy and has to be done slowly and with care. Initially I use a freshly sharpened, curved cabinet scraper—this allows me to scrape away exactly where it is needed and removes material relatively quickly due to the small area of contact. Work in a variety of directions but always ensure that you work in from the edges and you do not allow the scraper to over-shoot the mother-of-pearl and dig into the surrounding veneer—one false move and you could have a nasty gouge which would be difficult to get rid of later.

73. When satisfied, apply a coat of 50/50 shellac sanding sealer (SSS)/French polish (FP)—see section on French polishing.

Fitting Hinges

74. Refer to Project 1, the Diskette Box, pages 33 and 34, to see how to do this.

Fitting the Cherry Lipping

75. Now complete the grooves to take the lippings at the front corners of box and lid by cutting into the corners with a scalpel and straightedge and removing the waste by chiseling.

76. Prepare the pieces for the lipping to the cross-section in the plan and cut the three pieces slightly overlength and miter. Cut a shallow shoulder at the back ends of the side pieces so that they slot in place into the back ends of the grooves as shown and miter the front corners.

77. Glue the pieces in place supported by bits of ¹⁄₁₆" ply flexed in place side to side and front to back as shown.

78. The back ends of the sides of these pieces now need a bit of careful shaping to accept the hinges: Chisel the backs of the lippings flush with the edges of the box for the length of the stay arms and then widen the recesses so that the stay arms slot into place. Glue small cherry blocks at the end of the lipping groove in the lid under where the hinges fit.

79. Now the box is ready for finishing. I applied several coats of 50 percent SSS and 50 percent FP, which I brushed on, sanded flat, eventually sanded with 1200-grit wet and dry paper, smoothed with 0000 wire wool, and waxed.

Refit the hinges to make sure that the box opens and closes easily—you may need to sand the outer edges of the lipping a little so that the lid is not too tight. The box is ready for lining.

Lining

80. I lined this using a dark green moiré—see how to do this in Project 3, the Jewelry Box, page 57.

75

76

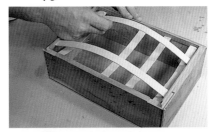

77

78

79

80

5 REMEDY BOX

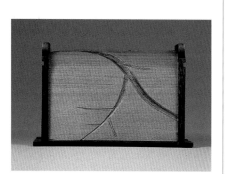

This lidded Bach remedy "tray" features a lid made from a laminated "tunnel" of veneers, carved away to reveal other colors, perhaps reflecting a Japanese influence. The construction is relatively simple but you will need to make the form to laminate the veneers onto. Choose colors appropriate for what you have in mind or you could, of course, choose to do this with natural timbers—I elected for the bold, colorful effect as usual. You should not carve to a depth of more than half the thickness of the lid, about 3/16", so the inner layers can be anything straight grained and flexible you may have on hand. Note that the grain runs the length of the box so that the pieces of veneer are actually wider than they are long.

If you are used to carving, this bit will present no problem. If you don't trust yourself to carve anything, then channels can be cut using the router table and a radius cutter—make sure you are able to hold the lid steady as you make the passes. Or you could use a mini-drill with a suitable attachment to "engrave" a design but you might find that the dust this generates will give a rather muddy effect, particularly if you are using any light-colored veneers.

All grooves are cut full length and show at the ends of the end pieces of the lid and the elements of the tray, adding a bit of extra interest.

The tape for binding when the veneer is being laminated can be any strong, woven tape—I used a good quality cloth bicycle handlebar tape.

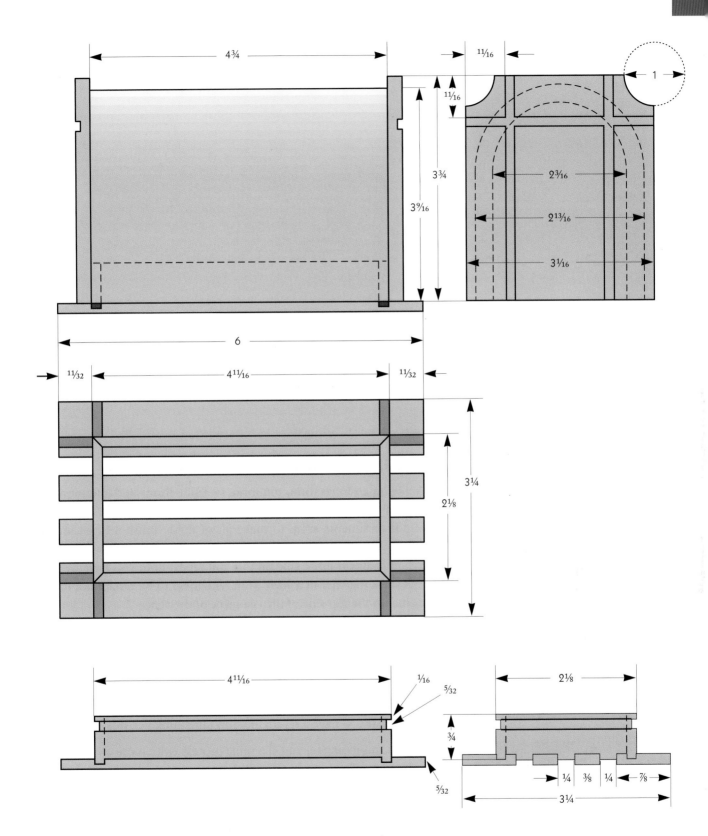

ELEMENT	MATERIAL	QTY	LENGTH	X x Y
BASE				
LONG SIDES	Ebony	2	$4^{11}/_{16}$" *	¾" x $5/_{32}$"
SHORT SIDES	Ebony	2	$2^{1}/_{8}$"	¾" x $5/_{32}$"
WIDE SLATS	Ebony	2	6"	⅞" x $5/_{32}$"
NARROW SLATS	Ebony	2	6"	⅜" x $5/_{32}$"
LID				
ENDS	Ebony	2	3¾"	$3^{1}/_{16}$" x ¼"
TUNNEL	Various Dyed Veneers	15 §	5"	8¾"

§ The actual number is not important but the grain must run along the length of the tunnel so the pieces of veneer will actually be wider (across the grain) than they are long.

Making the Tunnel

1. Make up an inner form, top form, two side forms and a tension bar—you can see these clearly pictured in Steps 2, 3, and 4. You can use mdf or suitable scrap to make all of these. Brush 15 percent diluted pva onto a piece of the veneer 5⅛" x 7½" and place another piece on it. Brush more glue on this and repeat until you have five pieces stuck together in a stack. (But remember to be careful not to put glue on the top side of the last piece of the veneer.)

2. Wrap the assembled sheets of veneer around the inner form and wind the cloth handlebar tape, or a similar tape, around this as tightly as you can, securing the end with masking tape. Now place the top form on top and the tension bar underneath, and clamp the whole works up firmly. Also take care to clamp the side forms in place so that you have a set-up looking something like this one.

3. Repeat this gluing up and clamping process twice more on top of the previous assembly and you will have produced a rigid tunnel of colored veneers, 15 sheets thick. Plane the ends of your tunnel square and level while holding the tunnel asembly in a vise with the form still in place, as shown. Then plane the bottom edges of this tunnel assembly straight and square, while the tunnel is held end to end in the vise.

4. You should make preparations for carving out the decoration that you want on the lid assembly of the remedy box. First lightly draw with a pencil whatever design you have created or decided on directly on the lid tunnel assembly.

5. Now you can go ahead and begin carving your design in the lid assembly. Take your time. It's best to keep clearly in mind as you carve that you need to avoid cutting too deeply. The best way to hold the tunnel while you are working on it is end to end in the vise, just as when you were planing the bottom edges. Apply some finish and set the lid tunnel assembly aside to dry.

Making the Ends and Base

6. You can use a template to mark the quarter circles in the upper corners of each of the end pieces. Cut these quarter circles out. With a sanding drum or similar tool, smooth the inside curves you've just cut in the end pieces.

7. Set up for work on the router. Cut all of the grooves using a 5/32" straight cutter. Remember to cut those that are across the grain first, as always.

8. Thoroughly smooth these end pieces after you have cut the grooves in them. Then you can apply your chosen finish to both sides of the end pieces and set them aside. When the end pieces are dry, smooth and wax them.

Check to see that the sides of your lid tunnel assembly are vertical and parallel. I found that the bottom edges of mine had flexed inwards very slightly as the whole assembly dried. To solve this, I used a couple of pieces of scrap to splay these out while the ends were being glued on. It is unlikely that you will find that the opposite has happened, but, if you do, a little pressure can be applied using a couple of small clamps to bring the sides in.

9. Before you actually glue them on, tape the ends to the lid tunnel assembly to check that all goes together as it should. Remove any finish from where the ends will be glued in place, and apply glue to the ends of the tunnel. Re-tape both pieces in place together with scraps of softwood and apply clamps as shown. When the whole lid assembly is dry, sand the bottom of the completed lid so that it is flush all around.

Be careful to be sure that the exterior dimensions of the vertical part of the base are 1/32" smaller than the internal measurements of the lid. It is best to measure the lid assembly's internal dimensions and then prepare the rest of the pieces accordingly. Cut the pieces for the base and ends exactly to these dimensions, but the pieces for the ver-

4

5

6

7

8

9

10

11

12

13

14

15

tical sides of the box should be left slightly overlength. This allowance on the vertical side pieces is so that the miters can be accurately worked to fit into the other pieces when all the grooves have been cut in them.

10. Take up the four pieces that will become the base and tape them together as a single unit, as shown. Then you can cut the necessary grooves across the ends of this assembly as though it were one piece. It will be necessary to hold this square against the router fence using a jig (refer to the notes on the "Router" and "Uesful Jigs & Aids," pages 11 to 13, and see especially the router "T" bar setup, page 12, for keeping pieces that need to be 90 degrees to the fence absolutely square and steady).

11. Disassemble and cut the grooves full length along the edges of the outer pieces, and leave the router set up. Work the miters to the two long side pieces. The best way to proceed is to saw first, then disc sand to exact length. That way the pieces can be formed so that they just slot into place in the two outer pieces of the base. Once you have achieved a snug fit, bring the two ends to their exact lengths. The decorative slots can now be cut along the outsides of the four pieces. Thoroughly sand all of these components. When they have been well-sanded, apply finish (be very careful not to get any finish in the sections of the grooves which will be glued), and set aside to dry.

12. Smooth these pieces thoroughly with 1200 wet & dry paper and 0000 wire wool. Apply glue to the slots in the two wider pieces of the base and to the miters.

13. After applying the glue, you can assemble the outside pieces that are part of the base. Secure the assembly with tape before you clamp it down.

14. Take this taped-up assembly and proceed to clamp it down onto a surface, as shown with a scrap block on top to distribute evenly the pressure of the clamp.

15. When the outer base assembly is dry, turn it over and glue the two inner struts in place. Be careful to glue these struts so that they are equally spaced. Once these last two struts are dry, you are ready to drill in from underneath to prepare pilot holes for the decorative brass pins. With a very light tacking hammer, gently knock in the fine brass pins. The pins should be placed one at each end of the narrow struts, and then three or four along each side. The last job is to snip off the heads of the fine brass pins, and file them flush to the surface of the box. This delightful little Remedy Box is complete and ready for use.

6 STUD BOX

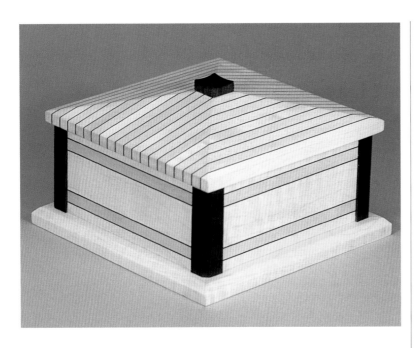

This is a very handsome but relatively simple box to make. Assembly does not require any complicated jigs or special equipment. The plan is completely square, which is unusual in terms of the projects in this book as well as most boxes that I make. I have chosen to use black veneer here because I like it and simply because I have used plenty of colored veneers elsewhere—but you should feel free to choose any color combination you like.

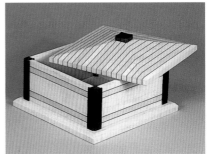

I have not lined this box—you could easily do so using a fabric fixed to card, but you will need to work it carefully around the ebony corners.

The dimensions given here are taken straight from the box I produced. The dimensions for the main box must be derived directly from those of the lid you have actually produced—a minute difference in the thickness of the veneer or the pieces you have used to make up the lid will have a marked effect on the final lid dimensions.

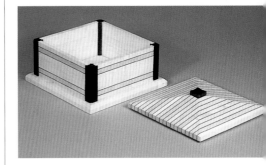

ELEMENT	MATERIAL	QTY	LENGTH	X x Y
LID	Maple	21*	5⅜"	1" x ¼"
	Black Dyed Veneer	20*	5⅜"	1"
FINIAL	Ebony	1	⅝"	⅝" x ¼"
BOX				
SIDES	Maple	4	4"	1⅞" x ¼"
CORNERS	Ebony	4	1⅞"*	½" x ½"
BASE	⅛" Birch Ply	1	½"	4½"
	Maple	4	5⅜"*	⅝" x ⅜"

*Depending on the thickness of your pieces—use as many as you need to produce the dimensions you want but remember to make any necessary adjustments to the plans.

1

2

3

Making the Lid

Once you have assembled all of the necessary tools and materials that you think you will need for making this Stud Box, you are ready to start. If you want to line this box; details on lining are given in Project 3, the Jewelry Box, page 57.

1. Take the wood you have selected for the lid, and prepare the pieces slightly overlength but to the correct width. Remember that where there is an asterisk (*) next to a measurement in the cutting list, it means that you should allow a little extra for trimming to length later.

Use one of these pieces as a template to cut out the veneer. Be careful as you cut each piece of veneer to cut it slightly overlength, as shown.

2. Glue all of the pieces together using full-strength pva. It is best to do this in two or more stages. First clamp several pieces firmly and ensure that you are setting up the pieces as level and square as you can. Then add more pieces to those already glued.

3. When this assembly is dry, you should choose one of the large faces of the completed square and then plane this face absolutely level. This level face will be the bottom of the lid.

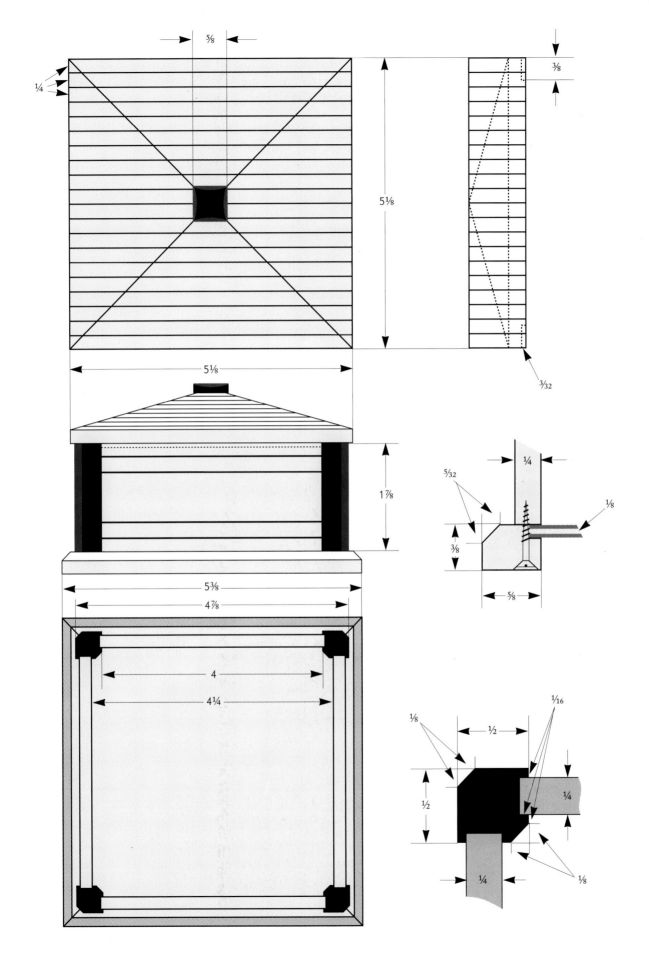

4

5

6

7

8

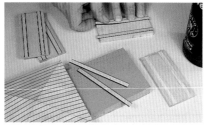

9

4. In order to ensure that the lid is an accurate square, measure across the grain—you may need to do a little planing to bring these edges exactly parallel.

5. Once this is achieved, then adjust the length (along the grain) to this same value by band-sawing and planing exactly square across the end grain to produce an accurate square.

6. Mark a line all around the edge 5/16" from the bottom and make a central mark at each end-grain end. Mark a triangle as shown in the plan and plane with the grain until you have removed the waste. If you have a band saw with sufficient height of cut, you can remove most of the waste first with this.

7. When you have planed down to the triangle marks at each end, make a mark midway along the top edge of the "roof" that you have created, and draw lines joining this point with each of the four corners.

Now remove these portions as well, still working with the grain, until you are down to the lines. You will have to set up a clever way of holding the lid firmly while it is angled upwards so that it is possible to do this planing. Ensure that the ridge that runs from the center to each corner terminates exactly at that corner. Be sure to check that you have planed down exactly to your marked lines all around the edges.

You should now have a symmetrical shallow pyramid shape—don't sand the faces; if your plane iron was good and sharp you should not need to do any sanding—do a little scraping if this is necessary.

Any sanding that you deem to be necessary can only be done after you have given the lid a coat of thinned sanding sealer and set it aside to dry. This will avoid getting dirty, black veneer dust in the grain of the light-colored maple. The lid is now complete except for the ebony cap and a shallow rabbet around the bottom to locate it in the box.

Making the Box

8. Take a piece of the maple 1" x ¼", slightly longer than your sides, and veneer both sides with the black veneer—or another color, or several if you like.

9. When this is dry, cut some ¹⁄₁₆" strips off it for the decoration around each side. Convert the four sides to the required dimensions and cut grooves on the router to take the decoration—these run off the ends which are hidden in the grooves cut in the ebony corners. Glue these in place.

10. Once these are dry, plane them flush, and give the pieces a coat of thinned sanding sealer. When the sealer is dry, apply a coat of full strength SSS. When that is dry, smooth with 1200-grit wet and dry paper and 0000 wire wool.

10

11. Convert the ebony to the cross-section in the plan, checking that the ends of your prepared sides fit neatly in the slots for them. Cut to length using a fine saw and reduce exactly to length by disc sanding to prevent breaking the grain at the ends. Do a trial set-up to check that everything goes together as it should. If satisfied, give the pieces a coat of thinned sanding sealer—these pieces will not need a full strength coat as ebony is very close grained and not absorbent. Smooth when dry, remove finish from any surfaces to be glued and glue up. I did this in two stages, gluing an ebony piece at each end of two of the sides, and then, when dry, joining them up with the other two. When dry, lightly sand the top and bottom edges of the assembled box flush and apply finish to the top edge.

11

12. Miter the pieces forming the lid "plinth" slightly overlength and then convert to the cross-section in the plan. Disc sand to the right dimensions to create a square 5⅜". Measure and cut a piece of ply to fit in the rabbet you have formed, glue in place and sand/plane flush.

12

13. Glue the main box in place on its plinth by clamping down onto the bench as shown using scrap to protect the upper edges. Drill, countersink and screw in from underneath using small countersunk brass wood screws. Ensure that the countersinks are deep enough so that the screws completely disappear.

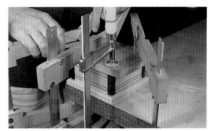

13

Fitting the Lid

14. Now work the rabbets around the bottom edges of the lid: Measure the internal dimension of the box and the full width of the lid. Subtract one from the other and divide by two. Set up the router so that the far edge of a wide, square cutter is just less than this value from the fence. Work across the grain first, then along it—you will then need to remove the corners of the square you will have generated on the lid's bottom as shown. Measure the diagonals corner to corner to check that you have removed enough. Increase the cut by tiny increments by reducing the overall size of the lid by planing two adjacent edges (one across and one with the grain, thus preserving squareness) and routing again. Keep going until it drops into place.

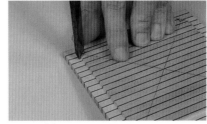

14

15. Chisel a flat area at the point of the lid as shown, and glue a small square of ebony or similar in place. Wax the whole box with clear furniture wax, buff, and your box is complete. You could line it if you wanted—see Project 3, the Jewelry Box, page 57.

15

7 MAP BOX

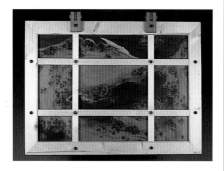

I have called this "Map Box" not because it is designed to hold maps, but because it looks like one, or rather, several. The beautiful yew I have chosen gives an effect startlingly like a map—yew is the best veneer I have come across for this, as it seems to encompass so many different figures, grains, and colors in a single piece.

You will need to decide exactly how you are going to divide up your lid. Where you are using consecutive sheets of veneer, reversing and/or changing the orientation of any nearly identical bits will help to maintain a random overall look to your "map."

The lid is the most important feature and I suggest you make this first allowing its dimensions to be dictated by the veneer you have available. The other dimensions can then be derived directly from your completed lid.

I wanted to keep the actual constructional work to a minimum with little thought for detail or finesse, other than on the lid—the nails and the hinges turned out to be a bit fussy, but apart from that the construction is certainly simple. I decided to rub-joint some pieces of pine together to create the required height for the front, back and sides, and to join them by gluing these to simple squares at the corners, each doweled for strength. I wanted to keep the fitting of the base as simple as possible so making up a simple L-shaped piece to fix it in place was the easiest solution. I knew roughly what I had in mind for the hinges, but somewhat dangerously (and I don't recommend this!) I decided to leave the details of exactly how these would work out until I had built the lid and could see how it sat on the rest of the box and then improvise.

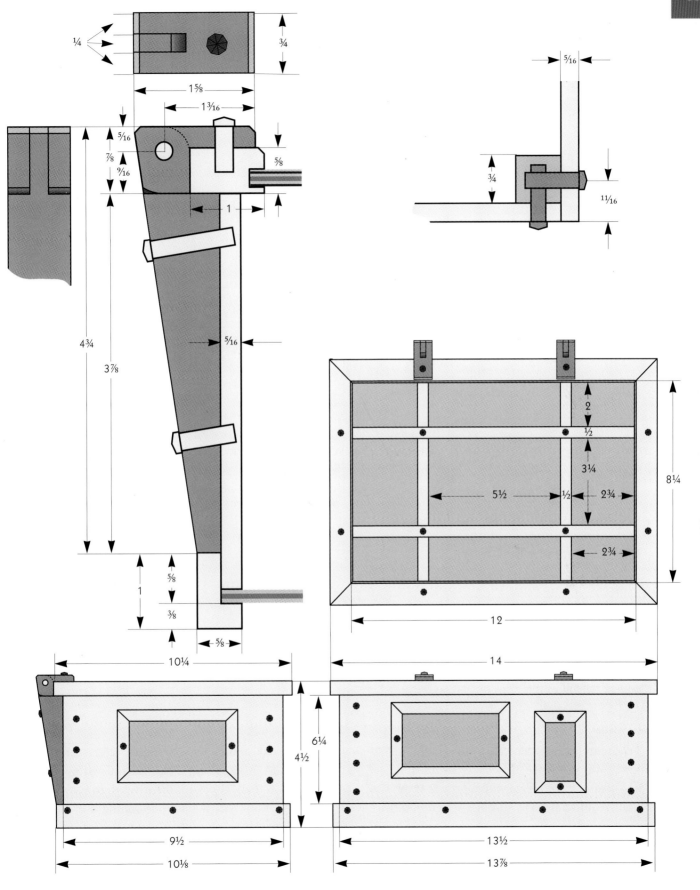

ELEMENT	MATERIAL	QTY	LENGTH	X x Y
LID	Pine	2	14" *	1" x ⅝"
	Pine	2	10¼"	"
DIVIDERS (also for Map Panel Frames)	Pine	-	12' approx.	½" x ¼" depending on how your lid and map panels work out.
BOX				
FRONT & BACK	Pine	2 §	13¼" *	⁵⁄₁₆" x 5"
SIDES	Pine	2 §	8⅞" *	"
PLINTH	Pine	2	13⅞" *	1" x ⅝"
	Pine	2	10⅛" *	"
BASE	⅛" Birch Ply	1	13¼"	9½"
HINGES				
MAIN	Cherry	2	5⅜" *	1¼" x ¾"
TOP	Cherry	2	1⅝" *	⅞" x ¾"
NAILS (incl. hinge pins)	Cherry	-	7' approx.	⁹⁄₃₂" x ⁹⁄₃₂"
VENEER	Well figured, waney-edged yew or similar, as available, for lid and map panels.			
	Blue dyed veneer for lid and map panels "background."			

§Depending on the width of stable board you have available you may need to rub-joint narrower pieces to achieve the full width.

I chose to make the dowels from cherry. The traditional way to make dowels is using a dowel plate—that is, a steel plate with a hole in it the size of your required dowels, through which you force slightly oversized pieces. There are many sizes of dowel available but I wanted to incorporate octagonal "heads" as if they were decorative nails. I started by making ¼" square-section pieces, converting these to octagonal by using a chamfer bit set up in the router. I then chopped these up into short lengths and then did a bit of trimming with a scalpel to remove the corners except at the "head" ends, which I wanted to leave octagonal and a little proud of the surface like old, handmade nails.

Making the Lid

1. Cut a piece of ³⁄₁₆" birch plywood slightly oversize for the lid and veneer it on both sides with blue dyed veneer. Experiment on the lid where you want your "dividers" to go—this will depend on what dimensions your chosen veneer will yield.

1

2. Once you have selected your yew or similar waney-edged veneer, shuffle your pieces around to create an effect that satisfies you. Trim the lid to size and the pieces so that they overlap the edges of your lid slightly. When you have flattened your chosen piece—see notes on flattening veneer in Project 4, Henry's Christening Box—and come to glue them in place, this should be done a few pieces at a time, starting with the largest pieces (these will tend to distort more if they are left for any length of time before they are laid down—the smaller pieces will distort less).

2

3. Apply 10 percent diluted PVA to the pieces to be laid down with a small, soft brush, working outwards towards the edges, avoiding building up glue around the edges which will squeeze out when pressure is applied, and tape the pieces carefully in place with masking tape. All flattened pieces should be stored under weighted boards until they are actually required.

3

4. When this is all dry, sand the surface well to remove any unevennesses, pencil marks, etc., in the veneer. Be careful not to allow the sanding block to dip and sand the background veneer, as this will also mean that you are sanding over the crisp edge of the yew.

You can do a little scraping if you feel that this is necessary, but again be very careful not to damage the weak, crisp edges of the veneer which give this whole project its character—keep any scraping to within the body of the larger pieces. It may well also be necessary to work carefully with a scalpel to remove any bits of paper that have glued themselves into any pits in the veneer and any glue that has seeped out from under the edges of the veneer, spoiling the clean edges. A No. 24 (curved) scalpel blade (with no handle) makes a good mini scraper, and can be very useful for this sort of operation.

4

5. When completely smooth, give both sides of the lid a couple of coats of sanding sealer or a two-part lacquer. When this is dry, smooth down to 1200-grit wet and dry and apply some good quality clear wax. When you come to put the lid together, any long areas around the edge of the lid which don't have any of your figured veneer on will require a fine strip of veneer glued along it so that the lid fits snugly into the groove along the inside edge of the lid frame. Similarly, the struts that go across the lid may need to be supported where there is no veneer underneath.

5

6

7

8

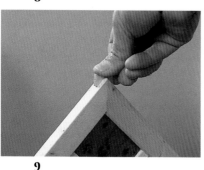

9

10

Measure the four pieces for the lid frame as shown in the plan and carefully miter these. (Following the general rule of doing operations across the grain before those with it, always do the mitring operations before cutting the grooves.) Then cut the grooves to exactly fit the thickness of your prepared lid—carefully widen a slightly undersized cut by adding masking tape to the fence.

6. Remove any wax and finish from along the lid edges to the depth of the groove and assemble with masking tape to check that it all fits together. When satisfied, glue up. Plane the corners flush and clean up the whole frame.

7. Cut the pieces for the dividers to length. The best way to bring these pieces exactly to the correct length is by using a disc sander (with a reliable 90° fence) to gradually shorten them until they just push into place. Check that all elements are going in completely square and when you are satisfied that all the pieces fit, smooth and apply some finish to the edges only of these pieces and set aside. Smooth and wax when dry, remove any wax and finish from under the pieces, and glue in place (you should not need to apply any pressure). When these are dry, sand the joins flush, smooth down to 320-grit garnet, and apply some finish to the top surfaces; smooth and wax as before.

8. I have cut some ³⁄₁₆" pine miter keys into the edges of the corners of the lid frame to add strength. To do this really neatly I have used a router and a miter-key cutting carriage (see "Jigs & Aids," page 13). You could cut these in by hand using a fine tenon or dovetail saw. Be sure to mark them out carefully first.

9. Apply glue and push these in place. Remember that the grain of the keys must always run across the corners and the keys should be trimmed from the corners inwards.

Making the Box

Measure your lid and plan to make the box ¾" smaller, that is, allowing for a ⅜" overlap all round.

10. Convert your pine to the required dimensions, edge-jointing to create the width you require and planing flush when dry. Cut these pieces to length, remembering that the sides should be shorter than the required front/back measurement by twice the thickness of the pieces.

11. When front, back and sides are prepared, glue ¾" pine squares to the inside ends of the sides as shown.

12. When dry, plane the ends of these pieces exactly flush and square.

13. Glue the front and back to these. Do this last part in three separate operations: one end to the front, the other to the back (being sure that you are gluing both together absolutely square) and finally the two assemblies together.

11

14. When dry, carefully plane and sand the ends, top and bottom completely flush and level—remember, your tools must be very sharp—and give the whole box a thorough sanding.

15. Cut a piece of ¼" birch plywood slightly undersize, sand thoroughly, apply finish, smooth and wax. Remove wax and finish from the glue area and glue it in place on the bottom. Make up four pieces of the L-shaped moulding to the cross section shown in the plan—these will form the plinth which covers the join between box and base. Notice the batten clamped in place to support the pieces being worked after the waste has been removed.

12

16. Place the box with base towards you with a long side uppermost. Cut a clean miter at the left hand end of a long piece, place in position, mark for the right hand end and cut this. When satisfied that you have a perfect fit, apply glue and tape it in place. Cut and disc-sand the left hand end of the next piece, and butt this against your already fitted piece. Mark, cut and sand the other end, apply glue, and tape in place. Continue working counter-clockwise around the base until you have fitted all four pieces (take particular care to fit the last piece accurately). Set aside to dry.

13

Making and Fitting the "Nails"

First convert your wood to ¼" squares (band saw and planer is by far the easiest way) and set up the router table with a chamfer (45 degrees) cutter. Adjust the height of the cutter very carefully so that you will be producing genuine octagons. You are unlikely to be able to achieve this with sufficient accuracy without a screw height adjuster, although with a chamfer cutter you can also adjust the effective height by adjusting the position of the fence.

14

17. To produce the individual nails, first set your disc sander fence to approximately 65 degrees and form an octagonal point on the end of one of your prepared pieces by offering it up to the disc gently eight times, once each with the piece lying on each of its eight faces. My sanding disc was a little worn when I did this job and it tended to scorch the end grain of these pieces slightly, but I decided to go with this as it added to the contrast with the pine.

Now set up a fence on the band saw to produce nails 1" long. A small three-wheel bandsaw with a fine blade is best—roll the pieces as you are doing the cuts to avoid breaking out the grain.

15

16

17

18

19

20

Alternatively you could use a dovetail saw that will not split the grain away at the end of the cut. It is worth setting up your band saw and disc sander so that they are close to each other, because this is a fairly repetitive process. Don't be too fussy about getting absolutely accurate, eight-faced points or you will be there all day!

Continue until you have the required number of nails—I allowed enough for the corners of the main box, around the plinth, two for each of the mini map panels, some for the lid, four for the hinge pins and a few spares—they soon add up.

You will need shorter nails for the plinth, for the lid, and for fixing the mini-panels in place and a couple of longer ones for fitting the hinges in place.

18. The next stage in the manufacture of these nails is to make a firm cut with a scalpel or craft knife ⅛" from the head end by rolling it on the work surface. With a little practice you will get very good at doing this and be able to make the cut join up with itself.

19. Now hold the piece vertically, head uppermost, and trim downward to remove the corners so that the cross section becomes nearly circular. Since these are going into low grade pine, which is very soft and forgiving, it is not necessary to do too much of this trimming work because these nails will drive home fairly easily anyway.

20. Reverse and trim up underneath towards the head, forming a shoulder to stop the nails going in too far. Finally, taper the non-head ends on the disc sander by twisting between thumb and forefinger. (Long live the disc sander!) It is worth doing a few trial nails first just to test your technique—most important is to get the amount of trimming work to the main nail just right so that you arrive at a good, snug fit, but not so tight that it splits the pine—have a piece of scrap pine handy with a few ¼" test holes in it. This is a fairly lengthy task, but keep at it and you will soon have them all done.

21. Mark out and drill holes, using a "lip and spur" bit, to take your nails. Be careful not to drill too deep and break into the inside of the box. Apply glue to the holes and carefully knock the nails home with a hammer using a piece of the pine to protect the heads. Don't knock them in too far otherwise you may split off a part of the head. You will not need to cut grooves in these nails as you would traditionally do with dowels because their trimmed cross section will be uneven enough to allow excess glue to distribute itself. The nails on the lid are shorter and purely decorative so a snug, push fit is sufficient for these. Remember not to fit nails along the back edge where the hinges will be fitted.

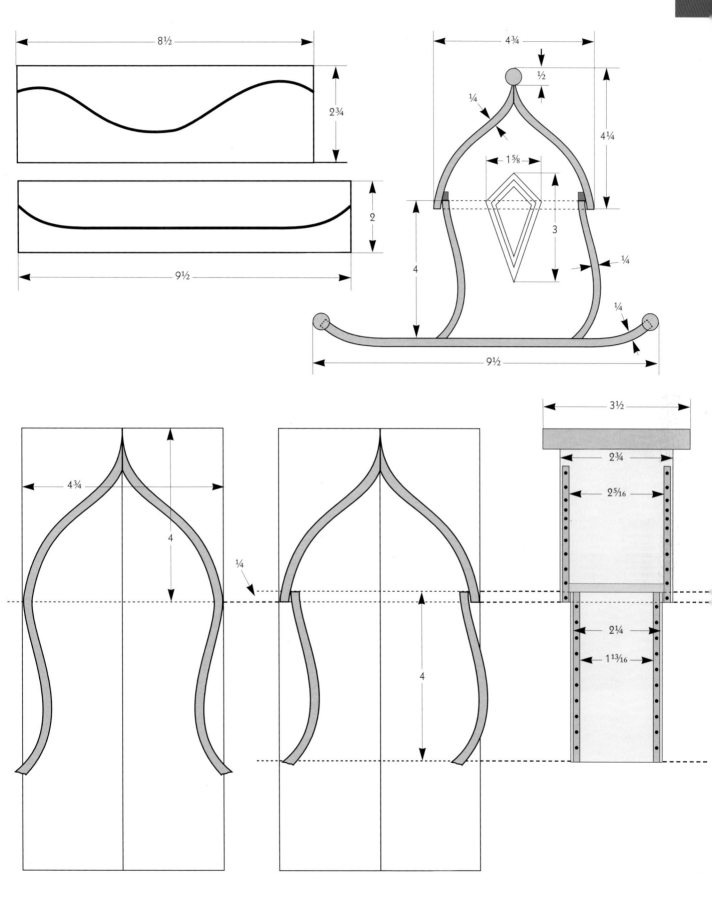

ELEMENT	MATERIAL	QTY	LENGTH	X x Y
SIDES & BASE	¹⁄₁₆" Birch Ply	9	10"	3"
FRONT & BACK	⅛" Birch Ply	2	8"	5¼"
VENEERS				
SIDES & BASE	"Douka" or Similar	6	10"	3"
FRONT & BACK	"Douka" or Similar	4	8"	5¼"
DOWELING	Ramin or Similar	3	3½"	½"
PLUS	Fine brass pins	(100–150)		

1

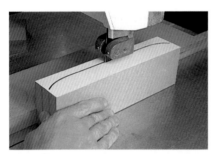

2

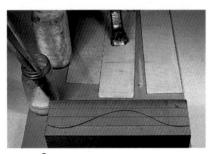

3

Preparing the Laminations

1. Cut out the shapes for the forms using a band saw. I used a fence in order to cut the straight portion of the form for the base; put this in place after cutting the curved portion at one end and remove it to cut the final curve—make sure that this straight line is exactly parallel to the square edge of the form, otherwise your cut will deviate from your drawn line.

2. Cut all the ply pieces for the sides and base slightly oversize, and apply glue to two of the pieces for the sides.

3. Clamp up all three firmly in the form. Fixing one large clamp in a vise, as shown, is a good way to get started with this sort of clamping operation—place the set up in the jaws of this clamp, tighten, and then the whole assembly is held firm and you have both hands free to apply the other clamps. When dry, repeat to produce the other side and the piece for the base. Veneer both sides of all three pieces with your chosen veneer in the same forms but using carpet underlay to ensure evenly spread adhesion.

Now plane the edges of your side pieces absolutely level and square, removing any rough-sawn edges and ensuring that both pieces are identical in width. Using the same form, veneer the inner and outer faces of both sides. Set up in exactly the same way, but using some carpet underlay between the veneer and the form on the inner and outer faces to ensure a completely even spread of pressure and, therefore, adhesion. Similarly veneer the other side and base.

Main Construction

4. Form the acute angles at the top of the sides on the disc sander—I have a partial fence at the back of the sander to take one end of the sides while the other end is being formed.

5. Glue the two sides together by clamping down flat onto the bench. I made a couple of shaped clamping pieces faced with 240-grit garnet paper to stop any slipping, as shown.

6. Now the assembled sides and base need to be faced with veneer. I clamped the base onto the bench on its side with some mount card underneath, and veneered the front and back of the side assembly at the same time in the veneer press, again using some mount card.

7. Trim off the excess veneer being mindful of the grain direction—try to trim so that the grain is leading the blade away from edges. Remember, also, that the assembled sides are still quite delicate, joined as they are only by glue at the apex miter. Veneer a piece of ⅛" birch ply on both sides with your chosen veneer, enough to yield front and back of both lid and base. Sand thoroughly, apply finish and smooth when dry. Use the best pieces for the outer faces. Now the lid is separated from the box and you need to determine exactly where the sides are vertical and make the cuts there: Measure the maximum outside width across the bulge and draw two parallel lines on a sheet of paper that distance apart, another line midway between them and another joining them square across one end.

8. Lay the assembled sides on this sheet between the parallel lines with a centerline through the apex. Make a mark on the sides where the parallel lines form a tangent with them. This may be a slightly different distance from your top, square line for each side—select the smaller value and mark a line square across at this distance from the top. Mark from this line onto both sides, and complete these lines square across each side. Don't throw away the piece of paper—you will need it again. Cut these portions off on the band saw with the assembly held flat on the band saw table with pieces of scrap ply underneath and at the back to prevent breakout.

9. Return to your piece of paper again and mark a line square across ¼" above the line drawn where the top half of the box was cut off. Place the "lid" onto your piece of paper again and position the two bottom pieces closer together so they fit just inside the top with their top edges on the new, higher line as shown. I have reversed one of the sides, but do as you like. Mark around the inner edges of both pieces in your chosen orientation, and draw a further line parallel with the cut-off line flush with their bottoms. Transfer this shape to a piece of your veneered ply and cut out.

4

5

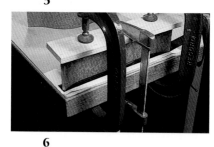

6

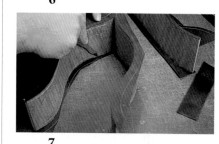

7

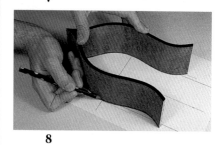

8

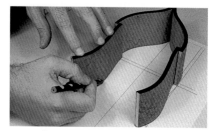

9

10

11

12

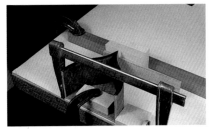

13

14

15

10. Mark through the assembled lid onto the insides of the veneered pieces for front and back with a sharp pencil, and cut this out as accurately as you can. Due to the possible slight asymmetry of the sides, it is important to work and fit front and back separately and mark which is which.

11. Smooth the curves back to the lines, first the convex lines on the disc sander and then the concave ones with a drum sander. Alternatively, do this using shaped sanding blocks being careful to keep the edges square. In any case, keep checking the fit and, when satisfied, give both sides of each piece another coat of finish and set aside to dry.

12. Clamp your prepared piece for the front of the lid, outer face down, onto a surface on a smaller scrap of /°" birch ply or similar— this will ensure that the front will be inset by a consistent amount all round. Offer up the lid assembly—check it is the correct way round—and clamp a batten onto the bench across the top of it so that you can place some scraps and a wedge to apply pressure to the apex to hold the pieces together as shown. You may also need to apply a clamp across the bottom. If satisfied with this set-up, disassemble, reassemble with glue and repeat for the back.

When dry, measure the internal front-to-back depth and reduce the sides of the box to this measurement. Plane the newly sawn edges completely level and square so that the pieces are the lid depth less /°" and re-lip these new edges to match the others by clamping down sideways onto the bench as before.

13. These pieces are glued to the front in a similar manner to the assembly of the lid. Clamp the shaped piece outside down onto the bench (on a scrap of ply), and clamp a batten on either side of this so that you will be able to apply pressure just where you need it. Common sense will dictate the exact shape and size of these pieces but do make sure that they are exactly square edged so that the pressure they are exerting doesn't push the curved pieces out of vertical.

14. When this has dried turn it upside down and place it on your other prepared, veneered piece. Mark the shape of the back as accurately as you can with a sharp pencil. Cut this out and shape as before, regularly checking the fit. When satisfied, apply glue to its edges, put in position and tape up to apply pressure. Use a scrap of 1/16" ply to ensure that the inset is the same as with all other pieces.

15. When this assembly is dry, sand its top and bottom edges flush and lip its top edge with the black veneer clamped upside down onto the bench. Carefully trim around this, taking particular care with the inside.

Fitting Pins, Base & Decoration

16. When dry, smooth and lay out for the pins: Stick a piece of masking tape along the front and back edges where the pins will be and using a marking gauge mark a line ¹⁄₁₆" + ⅛" (= ³⁄₁₆") in from these edges. Make some equally spaced marks, ⁷⁄₁₆" apart, along a piece of card and use this as a guide to lay out the positions for the pins, starting ³⁄₁₆" from the bottom end to the edges. Mark first with pencil, then with the point of a scriber, and remove the tape. Apply finish to the sides of lid and base, including all lippings. When dry, smooth and drill all holes for the pins in the lid. Clear the waste from the bit at least once for every hole. If you don't it can build up pressure so that you are not actually drilling at all and you can break the drill or split the ply.

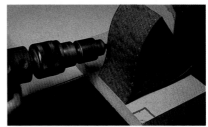

16

17

17. To hammer in the pins, I just placed the opposite corner of the lid on a piece of scrap softwood to avoid damage and hammered away ensuring that I was holding the lid steady. Take this slowly and carefully, however, because until the pins are in place the lid is still only edge-glued together. Measure, mark, drill and fit pins into the base exactly as with the lid, but don't fit any pins to the top ¼" because this will interfere with the lid.

18

18. Decide exactly how you want your box to sit on the base. Mark out with masking tape and glue it in place, clamping down onto the bench using a piece of scrap to protect the top edge. Screw this in place from underneath using deeply countersunk fine wood screws.

19. Glue a narrow strip ³⁄₁₆" x ³⁄₁₆" inside each side of the lid, ¼" up from its bottom edge so that it will sit securely on the box.

19

20. Cut out three different colored diamond shapes as in the plan (or design your own) and laminate these together taped down on a small setting-up board. Cut this in half and glue the pieces to the front of lid and box so that they line up—this will mean that the top edge of the bottom half will need to be ¼" below the top edge of the front of the box. Remember to remove finish from the glue area.

20

21. Prepare three pieces of ½" hardwood doweling, each 3½" long. Cut to length on a small band saw, rolling to prevent breakout and disc-sand the ends square. Hold in a vise as shown and carefully cut out a slot in each, one to take the point of the lid and the other two to take the ends of the base. To cut the sides of the slots parallel place the dowel low in the jaws of the vise and cut using a scalpel along a straightedge or similar held against the nearest jaw. When you have a snug push fit for all three pieces dye them black. Wax the box, rubbing all over with 0000 wire wool and buff with a duster to a warm, lustrous finish.

21

9 HARLEQUIN BOX

I have made this box in plain American black walnut, a good wood for box making as it is light, usually very straight grained, and works easily. I wanted to make this box relatively high in order to help to disguise the false bottom and have placed it on feet to further contribute to the confusion about height. I did not have a sufficient width of quarter-sawn stock to make up the height of sides that I wanted so I edge-jointed some narrower pieces.

I wanted to do the comb joints on the router but I don't have one of the many commercial jigs available—neither do I have a table saw. If you have either of these, form the joints in your usual way. If you don't, you will need to make a jig—see "Useful Jigs & Aids," pages 12 and 13—and have a router cutter the exact width you want your "fingers" to be. You will also need a supply of spacer strips exactly the thickness of the router cutter.

To produce the five panels required for this decoration I edge-glued five strips of dyed veneer 6" x ½" with thin strips of black veneer in between each and cut across these at an angle of 30° to yield eight diagonal strips of five diamonds per panel. These were then joined, again with the black strips in between, to produce the panels from which I cut the final strips.

The black lines between the colors can be a bit of a problem—in the past I have used commercially available ⅟₃₂" black dyed squares and have often found that the black dye has not reached the center. This means that when you scrape back the slightly proud lines between your colors you arrive at a sort of dirty mid-gray and not

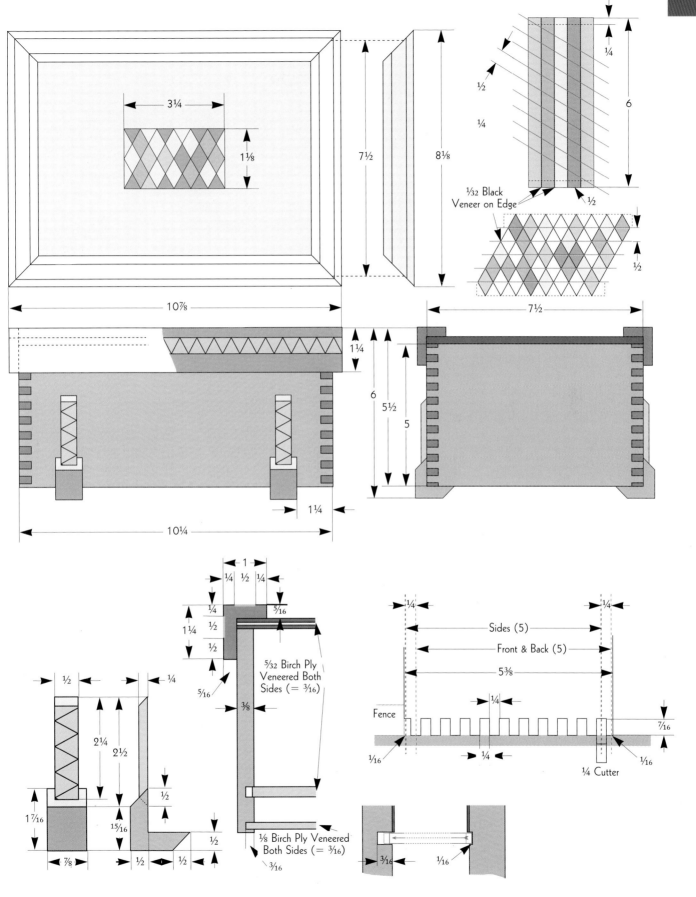

ELEMENT	MATERIAL	QTY	LENGTH	X x Y
FRONT & BACK	American Black Walnut	2§	10¼"*	5⅜" x ⅜"
ENDS	American Black Walnut	2§	7½"*	5⅜" x ⅜"
LID FRAME	American Black Walnut	2	10⅞"*	1¼" x 1"
	American Black Walnut	2	10¼"	1¼" x 1"
FEET	American Black Walnut	1	6"	1¼" x ⅞"
"BUTTRESSES"	American Black Walnut	1	12"	½" x ¼"
LID	³⁄₁₆" SuperPly1§§	1§	10¼"*	7½"*
BASE	⅛" Birch Ply	1	9⅞"*	7⅛"*
FALSE BASE	³⁄₁₆" Birch Ply	1	9⅝"*	6⅝"*

*As always, the asterisk indicates that you should allow a little extra for trimming to length later.

black. Real ebony might seem to be a solution but so far as I know this is not available in ¹⁄₃₂" squares. It is available in ³⁄₃₂" squares but this is really too large for this sort of work. The thinnest ebony veneer commonly available is ¹⁄₁₆" thick and with good reason: ebony can be pretty wild when it gets thin and this, combined with its brittleness, can make it virtually unusable.

My solution is to use thin strips of black dyed veneer turned on edge. This is a bit fussy to cut and use, but it is always completely black through its thickness, and its scale—¹⁄₃₂" thick—is also correct to produce a well balanced effect for small harlequins such as these.

In order that the false bottom should function, you need to fit a spring at one end to keep the base in the slot at the other. I have used a piece of a spring from a old car seat-belt mechanism. If you ever need a spring for a more rugged application, piano pedal springs are ideal and available from any piano restoration company or parts retailer.

Making the Base & Lid

Cut pieces of ³⁄₁₆" birch ply for the base and lid. If you have made up some ³⁄₁₆" "SuperPly," that is ideal for this. It's not necessary to have SuperPly, but see Project 2, the "Backgammon Board," for a description of this material. Veneer both the base and the lid with good straight grained walnut or to match whatever solid you are using. Ensure that the grain of the walnut is running the length of both panels and across that of the face veneers. Make the piece for the lid about ½" oversize so that this will also yield some scraps of the correct thickness for using to raise the lid housing components when they are being glued in place.

1. If you are using a standard jig to do the joints then prepare your timber for the four sides as necessary, follow your normal routine and jump to step 4. If not, prepare the timber for the sides about ¼" over width, exactly to length, and proceed as follows:

ELEMENT	MATERIAL	QTY	LENGTH	X x Y
VENEERS				
LID	Walnut to Match Solid	2	10¼"*	7½"*
BASE	Walnut to Match Solid	2	9⅞"*	7⅛"*
COLORS FOR	Dyed Veneers	5 x 5 §	6"	½"
PLUS:	Springs, screws and lining materials			

§Depending on the width of stable board you have available you may need to rub-joint narrower pieces to achieve the full width.
§§See how to make this in Project 2, the Backgammon Board, or you could substitute a single piece of ³⁄₁₆" birch plywood.

2. Make the jig as shown from ¾" mdf—glue the right angle together, glue the triangles in place and then screw these in from both faces. The cutouts in the triangles are to allow the 3" clamps I used to fix the pieces being worked onto the jig to operate. Prepare the¼" spacer strips ¾" wide and the length of the jig (I have used pairs of ¼" strips to arrive at the same result). Clamp two pieces of scrap the same width as your prepared pieces to the vertical portion of the jig ensuring that the ends of the pieces are square and flush with the base and that the edges are against the fence. Set a ¼" square cutter into the table set to a height of ⁷⁄₁₆" (slightly more than the thickness of your sides). The distance from the near edge of the cutter to the fence should be the full width of your prepared pieces less ⁵⁄₁₆"—this set-up allows a little extra at the top and bottom to allow it to be planed flush after assembly.

Make three test cuts holding the jig firmly against the fence, the first with no spacer in place, the second with one pair of ¼" spacers and a third with two pairs. Remove the scraps from the jig, reverse one piece and fit the worked portion together to see if the repeat is working. I discovered I needed to "thicken" my pieces by one piece of masking tape each—this then gave exactly the correct repeat to yield a snug fit for all pieces.

3. When satisfied with your experiments, clamp up all four of your prepared pieces to the jig and make all necessary cuts, starting with all your spacing strips in place, removing them in pairs for each successive cut. Then reverse and make the cuts to the other ends start-

1

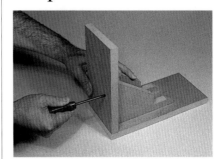

2

3

4

5

6

7

8

ing with one less packing piece. I wanted to keep both ends of each piece the same format—a half "finger" at each end of the long sides and a half cut at each end of the ends. In order to achieve this keep the same edge of all pieces towards the fence throughout the whole operation and when you come to make the second lot of cuts just flip the pieces end for end. This will result in each pair of pieces having identical cuts in each end. Reduce the pieces to their final width by band-sawing and then planing until all pieces assemble flush— the plan shows the orientations of the long and short pieces relative to the joints. Work grooves in the four sides to take the base by routing and in the two ends to take the false bottom. These grooves need to be different depths: $\frac{3}{16}$" at the closed end and only $\frac{1}{16}$" deep at the open end—just deep enough for the false base to safely slot into (it will be held in place by the spring acting from the other end).

4. Make the springs for the false base, one short and two long as shown in the photos for Steps 43 and 45. Work a tight curve in the acting end of each by bending the end over a piece of steel rod in a vise with the end held against it with a pair of pliers.

5. Chisel a cutaway as shown to house the short spring the same depth as the groove, and drill and screw it into place (preferably using a short machine screw). Notice that I have positioned this so that the end of the spring is acting on the center of the base panel(see photo, Step 43). The springs to lift the other end of the panel when it is slid across will be fitted when the box has been assembled and lined.

6. I have held the box together with 12 spring clamps while gluing up (these are old battery lead clamps) but there are many other ways to clamp up. This method requires eight pieces of scrap ply (two for each corner), grooved to take the "teeth" of the clamps to stop their slipping. They are clamped in position as shown. The big advantage of this method is that it is very quick to use—just apply the glue to the joints, assemble and apply the clamps. I always use slightly thinned pva for this sort of joint as it slows the drying time a little. However you hold the box together, always check to see that the box is exactly square—this joint is not particularly good at holding itself square. Either do this by checking inside with a set square or measure the diagonals, which should be identical. Any discrepancy can be corrected with a bit of tape fixed diagonally—the exact treatment will suggest itself.

7. When dry, sand top and bottom edges absolutely flush and sand all joints level. Give all external surfaces a couple of coats of finish and sand smooth when dry.

Making & Fitting the Lid Housing

8. Cut the veneered piece for the lid to exactly the external dimensions of the box. Cut four pieces of 1" x ¼" walnut ½" overlength and cut out the rabbet from these for your lid housing.

9. Blocks with strong springs attached to them clamped to the table hold the pieces you are working on firmly in place during passes as shown. Notice also improvised chip/dust extraction—this is important because this operation produces plenty of both. This is quite a lot of material to remove and I suggest you do it by routing in two or three easy stages, not cutting the full depth of cut initially. If you have a table saw make two cuts to remove most of the waste first and trim down to the exact values on the router or using a rabbet plane. Measure the length and width of the assembled box and add to this twice the thickness of the vertical portion of the prepared lid housing edging and add about ¹⁄₁₆" to these values. Bring your prepared pieces to these lengths by band-sawing with a 45-degree fence, using a miter saw, or using a miter chopper/trimmer if you have one. Note that if you are using a miter chopper you must cut these miters with the housings upside down to avoid any splitting.

Now cut out the channels to take your decorative edgings using a square cutter on the router, gradually opening it out by adjusting the fence and/or adding masking tape, as necessary. These Channels should precisely accept your rule or template (see Step 14), and should be fractionally deeper than the thickness of your veneer strips. This is one case when it is best to inlay a decorative strip slightly deeper than its surroundings.

10. Disc-sand one end of a prepared lid housing piece. Place on the box so that your sanded end lines up with the corner of the box, make a mark on the inside of the vertical portion at the other end and disc-sand back to this mark.

11. Glue this first long piece in place using the scraps from the prepared piece for your lid to raise it to exactly the right height—a single piece of masking tape stuck to the bottom of each piece of scrap will ensure that there is just enough clearance to allow the lid to slide smoothly.

12. With the first long piece clamped in place you can then immediately proceed to measure, trim and fit the second. Work counterclockwise around the box and when you have fitted one short and two long pieces, clean any excess glue from where the lid will run.

13. Plane the lid edges until it slides smoothly into place, remove and give both sides a couple of coats of finish.

9

10

11

12

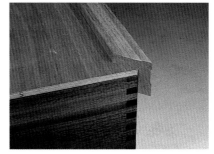

13

14

15

16

17

18

19

Making the Decorative Strips & Panel

14. Cut out six pieces of differently colored veneer—one must be black— each 6" by 1½" with the grain running along the length. I have used a ½"-wide steel rule, but note that whatever you use must have some abrasive paper fixed underneath to hold it really firmly where it is put—I usually use 240-grit garnet paper. Hold your chosen template along one edge of one piece and using a new, sharp blade remove the merest sliver to true up the edge.

Continue to hold the rule in position and swivel the veneer around and cut along the other side of the rule. Finish with one further fine cut, undercutting very slightly. This method should produce absolutely clean, straight edges and strips of a completely consistent width.

15. Continue until you have cut five identical strips from each piece (except the black) and arrange your colored strips so that you have five different combinations of five strips. I have omitted one color from each group and duplicated a color to make up for it.

16. Now cut the thin strips from the black piece. Don't measure these, just do them by eye—you will be using the strips on edge so the actual width of these pieces is not critical but should be only just wider than the thickness of the veneer. If the veneer is ¹⁄₆₄" thick then make the pieces just less than ¹⁄₃₂"—any wider and the pieces can crush under pressure. If they are being a little problematic and tending to tear out from under the straightedge, flip the piece over and cut so that the tendency is reversed. When cutting these slivers do so with minimum downward pressure, allowing the sharp blade to do its work. If you cut straight through in one go you are using too much pressure and could fracture the delicate veneer and will certainly cause it to curl, making it difficult to use. Two or three passes is much better and will not stress the veneer.

17. Tape a piece of waxed paper to the setting-up board—offcuts of ordinary melamine faced shelving make good boards for this sort of thing—and prepare the five strips with a piece of ½" masking tape across each end as shown. Tape one piece in place down one side of the waxed paper and brush glue along its inner edge.

18. Put a black strip in place and apply glue to the edge of this. Apply glue again, another colored strip, and tape in place. Repeat until you have laid down all five strips, place a sheet of paper and a piece of carpet underlay on top and put under moderate pressure in a veneer press or similar. Don't worry about using plenty of glue during this operation—whenever I do this job the waxed paper backing ends up with an almost complete covering of glue. It is better to use more rather than less because that will slow the drying time more. Keep a rag handy to remove any excess glue from the surface and to push the strips against the backing. Be careful that the black strips go into place in the correct vertical orientation—if they go in flat it will disrupt the spacing and will be uneven.

19. Remove it from pressure when dry and scrape the black lines down flush to give a completely smooth panel. The pale green veneer I used here was fractionally thicker than the others so a little extra scraping was necessary to bring it down level with the others.

20. Cut off the taped ends, and carefully remove the panel; scrape any excess glue from the reverse and hold up to a bright light/window to check the joins. You are bound to get the odd chink of light showing through but beware if you have whole lines that are barely joined at all—in extreme cases you will find that the whole piece will fall apart, which will definitely indicate that you need a bit more practice! It is well worth getting this right now because any problem at this stage will be multiplied later when the second generation strips are joined up! If all is well, repeat the whole procedure until you have five smooth, colorful, cleanly jointed panels.

21. Now form the second generation strips by cutting across these panels at an angle of 30 degrees.

22. You will get seven or eight pieces from each panel if you are working to the dimensions here. Do this in exactly the same way as cutting your original strips but be careful at the ends of the cuts because it is easy to pull off the bottom piece if any of the joints are even slightly dodgy.

23. Juggle these second generation strips so that you have no adjacent duplicated colors. Prepare your strips as before but with the tape diagonally across the ends as shown. In order that you don't have to make any difficult last minute design decisions while you are doing the actual gluing up, place the pieces on a piece of scrap in the order in which you want to lay them down.

24. Tape a single piece onto your setting-up board, at an angle this time, apply glue and continue to make up your panels as before. Don't try to lay down all eight strips in one operation but in two separate goes, four strips each time. This is better than battling to do all eight in one go and finding that the back of the panel is not flush because the glue hardened too much before you got it under pressure. I have used eight strips per panel yielding five panels in all.

25. When dry, remove the tape being careful not to lift the grain as before.

20

21

22

23

24

25

26

27

28

29

30

26. Scrape the panels flush working at a slight angle across the panels as shown.

27. Cut just inside the taped sections using a scalpel and straight-edge level with the points of the second diamond in each strip.

28. Removing these completed panels from the setting-up boards can be a little scary. If the joins are good the panels are surprisingly strong considering the minimal glue area and will not have adhered too strongly to their backing, but go carefully anyway working a thin, flexible rule or similar under the panel in order to release it from the waxed backing paper. Move the rule gently so that it is not parallel to the strips otherwise its movement may cause less than perfect joins to break.

29. The third generation strips are cut exactly as before but these are the most delicate of all. Being careful to still hold the rule exactly in place, swing the piece around—by moving the panel, not the rule—and repeat the two or three cuts on the other side to produce your final strip ready for inlaying into the lid housing. You will notice that there are a couple of incomplete pieces which parted as I was cutting the strips—this is bound to happen. In any case use gentle pressure so that you only cut right through on the third or fourth pass.

Fitting the Strips

30. Now take a bit of time planning the order of strips around the lid housings. The complete, unbroken lengths will not have black lines at the ends so use the shorter pieces to yield filler pieces with black lines at both ends to join the others. You will have to improvise at the corners a little and there is really no way to actually match the pattern there. Even if you try to maintain the pattern all the way round it will not match at the fourth corner. Glue your prepared strips into the channels along the lid housing using 10 percent diluted PVA brushed on with a small brush. Start from an open end and work in one direction only, otherwise you will find that your pattern will not match where it meets in the middle.

31. When all the strips are in place they must be scraped flush. This is not as easy as it would first seem because of the various grain directions involved. I found that working obliquely, as shown, was the safest way. You will, in fact, be scraping almost exactly across the grain of half of the black lines, which is why this operation is a bit tricky, but it should work out fine if you are careful.

Once you have achieved a near-perfect level surface for all the buntings, brush well with a fine, dry clean brush to remove all dust

and apply a coat of thinned sanding sealer and set aside. When dry, apply two coats of full strength SSS allowing it to dry between coats. Sanding, of course, is out of the question at the initial stages due to the problem of getting dirty dust in the grain of the colored veneers—however, once you have sealed the grain in this way a certain amount of gentle sanding can be safely done.

Making the Feet

32. These are produced from one piece of solid walnut with a cross section 1¼" x ⅞" cut as shown. Start by planing a piece accurately to size and mark a centerline down the 1¼" wide side. Cut two miters at one end to form a point as shown. Make a mark ¾" back along the center line—this will be the inside corner—and mark a pair of 45° lines, parallel to your original miters, meeting there as shown. Saw outside these lines, clean up the outside miters that are left on the parent piece by disc sanding or chopping and repeat the process until you have the four feet.

33. Clean up the inside miters with a bit of careful chiseling (the chisel must be sharp for this because you will be cutting obliquely across and into end grain) so that the feet fit neatly around the bottom edges of the box.

34. Carefully cut the short grooves in the top corners of the feet to take the "buttresses" with a narrow chisel. These grooves could be omitted, if desired, and the miter on the bottom ends of the buttresses reversed to fit snugly over the miters on the feet. The result will be little different but is somehow a less satisfying construction. Apply some sanding sealer and set aside to dry.

35. Make the buttresses by sticking strips of your leftover bunting, six complete colors long, to a single piece of walnut ½" x ¼" x 12". When dry, smooth the surface with some careful scraping, apply some finish and sand completely smooth as with the other bunting. Apply some full strength sanding sealer and set aside to dry. Smooth with 1200-grit wet & dry paper and 0000 wire wool, cut into pieces 2½" long and miter each end. Drill a hole through the underneath of each foot in readiness to screw them into the bottom edges of the sides—countersink deeply so that the screws are well recessed—and glue them in place equally spaced along the front and back of the box. Measure their positions carefully and remember to remove finish back to bare wood to ensure good glue contact. You will not need to clamp these in position in any way; just push them firmly in place and the glue will grab them firmly. When dry, drill through the holes into the bottom of the sides and screw in place.

31

32

33

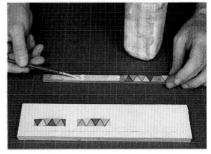

34

35

36

37

38

39

40

41

36. Glue the buttresses in place removing, as always, any finish from the glue area. Smooth the body of the main box with 1200-grit wet & dry paper and 0000 wire wool.

Fitting the Lid Panel

37. Tape the panel in place centrally on the lid (or wherever you want to place it) and use a fresh scalpel blade to cut around the outside, supporting the edge of the panel with a straightedge, as shown. This will, of course, cut through the tape that is holding it in place—cut both long sides first and then fit fresh tape before cutting the short sides. Remove the tape and reinforce the cuts with the straightedge placed outside the rectangle. Remove the veneer either by careful chiselling or by using a finely set router freehand.

38. I often use an old miniature "nag's tooth" plane to remove these areas for small panels. The blade is set to just the correct depth to remove the veneer and nothing else. This is the ideal tool for this job but you can't see the blade working so you must be particularly careful not to damage your neat, scalpel-cut edges. It will work equally well used across the grain so long as the sole is wide enough to span the whole area being worked wherever the blade is. In any case the extreme edges will need to be worked separately and I used a shallow gouge for this.

39. When the veneer is removed, check the fit, adjust if necessary, and glue the panel in place using some diluted PVA and place under moderate pressure in the veneer press or with clamps. When dry, scrape completely flush being careful, as before, with the angle of scrape.

Notice in the foreground the piece of ¼" ply with a 90° portion cut out of it which facilitates scraping operations such as this. Apply sealer, sand and smooth with 0000 wire wool.

Slide the lid in place so that its back edge is exactly flush with the end of the box. Most importantly it must be absolutely parallel to this edge—plane the edges of the lid slightly, if necessary, to achieve this. The front end of the lid should not quite make contact with the end of the housing—this ensures that the miters on the part of the housing that is connected to the lid fit snugly in place.

40. Put the final piece of housing in place at the back of the lid to finally check for fit and shorten and/or adjust the miters slightly on the disc sander if necessary. If satisfied, remove the lid again and remove finish from the area to be glued. Clamp onto a bench with ⅟₃₂" of the back edge overlapping and glue the piece in place, clamping gently in position. Apply glue to the back edge as well as to the top face of the lid and ensure that the housing is pushed up snugly against it. Use a piece of scrap softwood to protect the surface from the clamp.

Lining

41. Before fitting the false base the box must be lined: The long sides are the full height of the box but the two end panels only reach down as far as the top edges of the grooves for the false base.

42

42. I have used some dark green moiré formed over card faced with ds tape and stuck in place using a latex adhesive. (For more details on lining see Project 3, the Jewelry Box, page 57.)

43

43. The false base is removed by pushing down at the right hand end and then pushing it to the left while sliding the hand along to the left to reduce the resistance to the springs—the right hand end will then pop up, and the piece can be removed. Glue a couple of small blocks to the base at each end, level with the bottom of the grooves for the false base so that it doesn't fall into the bottom of the box when it is released. Notice that I have glued a block centrally at the spring end—this is slightly sloped up towards the end to guide the false base onto the spring.

44

44. Screw the two remaining springs onto small blocks using two screws each (to prevent them from twisting and interfering with the sides of the box).

45. Glue these into place along the sides of the real base, as shown.

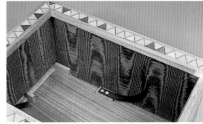
45

46. Measure the internal dimensions of the lined box, and cut a piece of ³⁄₁₆" plywood for your false base ¹⁄₁₆" less wide and ⅛" longer than these values. This will ensure that it is long enough so that when it's in position it doesn't pop up and short enough so that when you slide it to the left it does.

Cover the piece with your fabric. I used a single piece which was folded right over the ply and around both ends meeting halfway along bottom, all fixed in place with ds tape. I left about 1" extra which I folded around the sides and fixed underneath with ds tape after I had removed the corners.

46

47. Insert the false base into the box and adjust the springs. The end spring should be just strong enough so that the piece is held firmly in its slot at the opposite end but not so strong that it makes sliding the piece against it difficult. The upwards acting ones can be as strong as you like to ensure that the end of the false bottom lifts clear of the open end—this will need to be fed in and out under the two ends of the lid housing at the open end.

47

10 OLLIE'S CHINESE BALLS

This box holds a pair of Chinese Exercise Balls ("much prized for their ability to enhance the user's health and sense of well-being") made by the Boading Iron Ball Company in China. The original box that came with them has seen better days.

To draw an octagon, first draw a straight line, and another, halfway along, perpendicular to it. Bisect one of the 90-degree angles this creates, and draw this line right through the first intersection. Draw another line perpendicular to this one through the same intersection, and your four lines should now form a star shape. Draw a circle with its center at the center of the star, and draw straight lines to join up the points where the circumference intersects your lines—this should be a pretty accurate octagon.

To work the 67.5-degree obtuse miters needed to join the eight pieces together, I made a carriage to hold the pieces while making passes on the router using a square cutter—see the plan on the opposite page and the photo on page 12 in "Jigs & Aids."

I made up the ends from ply with a maple insert because it is more stable this way, but you could cut each end from a single piece of maple. The balls fit into circles cut out of a piece of ply. These are cut about 3/16" larger than the diameter of the balls, and the fabric is tastefully stuffed through the holes and down around the sides before the panel is fitted in place. Depending on the combination of material and wood, latex adhesive can work very well if it is applied sparingly to a prepared piece and pushed firmly into place immediately. I make use of ds (double-sided) tape in many steps.

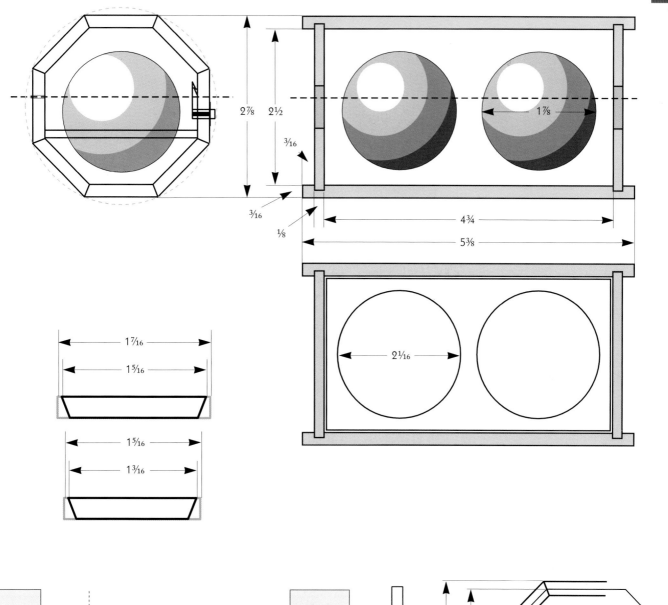

2⁷⁄₈

2½

³⁄₁₆

³⁄₁₆

⅛

1⁷⁄₈

4¾

5⅜

2¹⁄₁₆

1⁷⁄₁₆

1⁵⁄₁₆

1⁵⁄₁₆

1³⁄₁₆

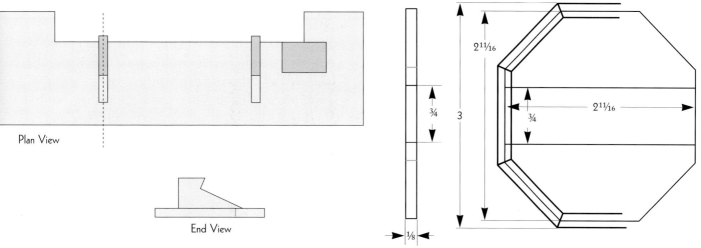

Plan View

End View

Obtuse Mitre Cutting Carriage

3

³⁄₄

⅛

2¹¹⁄₁₆

2¹¹⁄₁₆

³⁄₄

ELEMENT	MATERIAL	QTY	LENGTH	X x Y
SIDES	Maple, Figured or Plain	6	5⅜" *	5/16" x 3/16"
	Maple, Figured or Plain	2	5⅜" *	1 7/16" x 3/16"
ENDS	Maple, Figured or Plain	2	2 11/16" *	¾" x ⅛" *
	3/16" Birch Ply	2	2 11/16" *	1 1/16"
INTERIOR	⅛" Birch Ply	1	4¾"	2½"
PLUS:	5⅜" * fine brass piano hinge, screws, spring catch, lining materials			

*As always, the asterisk indicates that you should allow a little extra for trimming to length later.

Making the Main Box

Convert your timber slightly over-length and over-width. Band-saw roughly to thickness, preferably in lengths that will yield three or four pieces, and then plane (by hand or planer) to the final required thickness. This value will depend on what you decide to use as your hinge.

Sand both ends of each piece exactly square and identical in length on the disc sander. This operation is particularly important in this case because if they are not identical in length the grooves to take the octagonal ends will not line up when the box is assembled.

Now cut the cross-grain ⅛" grooves, 1/16" deep, to take the ends. You will need a 90° jig to hold the pieces square to the fence. Take it slowly to avoid breaking out the grain at the end of each cut.

1. Clamp a piece of scrap to the bench, slightly thinner than the groove, place the pieces on this as shown and cut away the fuzz around the cuts—this is a useful trick and makes cleaning up after routing operations quick and easy.

Now make up the carriage as shown in the plan on page 113—I started with a piece of ¼" mdf, cut out a section where the actual cutting would happen and fitted two angled supports with stops to hold the pieces. The size of the cutter is not important but it must be sharp and long enough to make the complete depth of cut. It is vital, when you have constructed the carriage, that you check that when a piece is in place ready to be cut it is exactly parallel with the fence. If not, adjust the angle by planing front or back of the carriage so it does run true.

2. Adjust the fence and the cutter height so that a pass will trim the edge of a piece to the desired angle. Work an angled edge to two pieces and check to see that they form the right angle. Correct by attaching bits of fine card to the front or back of the supports—common sense will suggest which way you need to correct. When satisfied, cut an angle down one edge of all pieces, making sure that they are placed on the carriage grooved (inside) face up, re-set the fence, and repeat for the other edges. Remember that you will need two different set-ups as you have to cater for the wider bits. Keep the router table scrupulously clean to avoid any chippings' getting caught between the carriage and the fence and causing inconsistencies in the cuts. When you have worked all your pieces, tape up and roll together to check for fit, remembering that the wider pieces should be opposite each other. If all is well, fine—if not, you may have to rework the pieces changing the angle slightly. If the outsides of the obtuse miters are open, you will need to "sharpen" the obtuse miter angle by raising the back ends of the pieces with bits of thin card stuck to the supports. Conversely, if the insides of the obtuse miters are open, you will need to "blunt" the angles by raising the front ends. In either case you will not need to re-set the router for the first lot of cuts, whichever way you need to correct it, but you will for subsequent cuts. Remove as little material as you can to preserve your planned dimensions but you should have a little leeway. Remember that you will need two different set-ups anyway to cater for the wider central pieces.

3. Now you need to make up the pieces for the ends: Edge-joint two bits of ³⁄₁₆" birch plywood and a piece of ³⁄₁₆" maple to make up a blank large enough for each end as shown. Use a scrap of the maple you have used for the body of the box which will be a little thicker than the ply. While this is drying, measure across one end of your taped up box, first at right angles to the wide bits and then parallel with them. This should give you two values differing by ⅛" if you have kept exactly to this plan. In any case, you now need to make a drawing of the shape for the ends—this will be an octagon, ³⁄₁₆" less all round than your external dimensions, with the two opposite longer sides for front and back.

4. Plane the pieces flush, mark and cut out these pieces—it is important that these are accurately made and especially are not too large because this will stop the miters' closing up properly when the box is assembled.

5. Re-tape the box and roll together with the ends in place to check for fit. If satisfied, disassemble and repeat with glue. I used full strength PVA for gluing the ends in their grooves and 10 percent diluted for the miters, brushed on with a fine brush. Undiluted PVA is quite thick and can sit in the joints, stopping them from closing fully. Remove the tape when dry, sand the ends flush being careful to preserve their squareness, and give the exterior a coat of finish. I have used a two part clear lacquer for this—a tough coating as this box is intended for travelling. I have used this thinned with some of its thinners as a first sealer coat.

Cutting off the Lid

6. Set up the router with a " square cutter and set up the fence so that you are cutting a groove along front and back of the box ¹⁄₃₂" short of full depth.

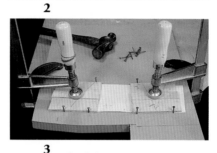

1

2

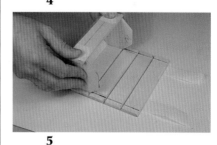

3

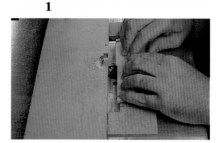

4

5

6

7

8

9

10

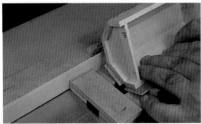

11

12

7. The position of this will vary depending on which sort of catch you have decided to use. I band-sawed the ends but you could do this by sawing by hand held in a vise—but clamp front to back, not top to bottom, or the box will collapse when you have cut through.

8. Cut through the final ¹⁄₃₂" with a scalpel.

9. Clean up the inner edges by careful chiselling, and sanding with the box halves face down on some 180-grit garnet paper using a gentle grinding motion. When both halves fit together perfectly finish off with 240- and then 320-grit garnet paper used with the grain.

Inlaying Lines along the Body

10. First make a couple of sandwiches using the colors you have chosen, with double black on each side, just longer than your box. With the edges of these prepared pieces planed straight and square now is the time to cut the grooves in the edges of the box to take the lines—it is easier to measure exactly the thickness of a line while it is still in this form.

11. Make a jig for cutting in the decorative lines similar to that shown in the photo. The actual construction is not crucial—I made this one from ¼" mdf and ¹⁄₁₆" veneer with the elements simply glued together. The angled pieces are covered with 240-grit garnet paper (fixed in place with ds tape) to hold the box firmly in place. Mark one edge and designate this as the edge to run against the fence. Cut all grooves—I have done these on the deep side, about ³⁄₃₂".

12. Plane both edges of your colored sandwiches absolutely square and straight and cut strips from both edges using a small band saw. Cut wide enough so that they will be proud when fitted in place to allow for trimming back flush—you will need only four of each color, eight in total. Glue these in place in your prepared grooves.

13. Trim the strips to length flush with the ends.

14. Then cut back carefully with a sharp, wide chisel level with the sides. Scraping is also useful for this but keep sanding to a minimum, just carefully rounding over the "ridge" of the lines and the corners at the ends. When you have arrived at a good level surface brush thoroughly to remove all dust and apply another coat of the thinned lacquer.

Fitting Catch & Hinges

First fit the main part of the catch, then the hinge, and finally the catch top plate. If you are not using this sort of catch, a study of the one you have chosen should suggest the best way to fit it.

15. Drill a hole to snugly take the button (not too tight, not too loose) dead center in the front of the box. Allow just enough of the catch to show so that it can be gripped by the lip to be fitted in the lid without the lip being too close to the edge of the lid's inner edge.

16. Widen this hole as shown to accept the retaining tabs from the front ring. Be careful not to make this slot wider than it needs to be otherwise this will show outside the front ring. Test in place and remove if satisfied.

13

Cut a rabbet along the back edges of the box half the depth of the hinge measured at the pin. Make test cuts on a couple of pieces of scrap to determine the correct setting. Cut a piece of the hinge slightly overlength with a piercing saw or fine hacksaw with the hinge held in a metalworking vise with wood on the jaws to avoid damage. Reduce to exactly the right length using the trusty disc sander and 90° fence. Mark along the length of the hinge where you want your holes to be—the more the merrier, but preferably about one every ½" to ¾".

14

17. A useful laying out trick is to cut a thin bit of paper ⅜" shorter than the length of your hinge and fold it in half end to end as many times as you need to until you have the spacing you want. Unfold the piece and the positions of the folds give you the spacing for your holes—transfer this spacing to masking tape stuck along the hinge for this purpose.

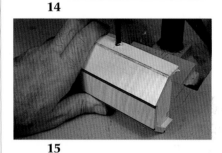

15

18. Set up your pillar drill/drill press with a simple stop to define the distance of the holes from the knuckle and drill away. Use a sharp drill fitted as deeply in the chuck as you can to avoid wobble and start the holes slowly, exerting only a little pressure at first to allow the drill to find a true center. Then, with all the holes drilled and the jig still in place, do the countersinking. Use a depth stop to avoid going too deep, otherwise the screws will pull themselves through the flap when you try to screw them in place—you don't have much thickness to play with.

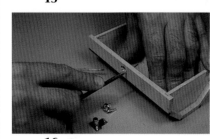

16

19. Clean up the holes and the underneaths of the flaps with a little gentle filing and polish up your hinge as in "Cleaning up Hardware," pages 20 and 21.

20. Drill and screw the hinge in place to the lid using a screw at each end and a couple of others.

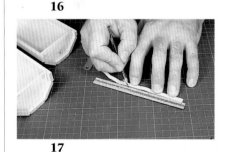

17

21. Fix the lid to the base using just two screws, and test to see whether lid and base line up. If they do, fine, if not (which is more likely) mark and drill a further two holes slightly off-center in the direction that the lid needs to move. Common sense will suggest what adjustments to make. Once lid and box line up exactly drill all

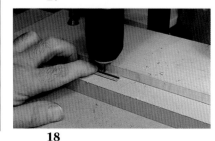

18

19

20

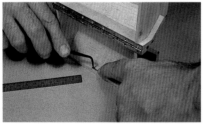

21

22

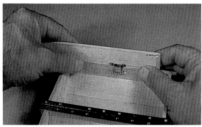

23

24

other holes dead center and fit the remaining screws. A little candle wax or similar will help these screws to run smoothly and will minimize the amount of force you have to use to screw them home, thus avoiding possible damage to the heads.

Make sure you remove all bits of brass swarf from the drilling surface before you drill any of the holes in the box to fit the hinge in place.

If at any stage you find that things are going horribly wrong and the lid and base are nowhere near matching up you may well have to plug some, or even all, of the holes you have already made. Use a piece of the same wood that you are drilling, about 2" long and ⅛" square, and use a scalpel or similar to reduce one end to a slightly tapered peg that will fit snugly into the hole you need to plug. Push it in place, score with the scalpel around the end of the peg level with the entrance to the hole (don't cut right through it) and remove it. Apply white glue to the hole, push the peg firmly in place and snap off at your score mark. This will dry quickly and you can mark and re-drill after about 20 minutes.

22. Put the main part of the catch in place but don't bend the tabs over yet. Measure carefully the distance from the box edge to the underside of the protruding part. Place a piece of scrap inside the front of the box and place the lip on it and measure as accurately as you can the distance of the holes from the bottom edge of the piece. It is best to actually fit the plate to the scrap to check that everything works as it should do—this takes a little longer but it means that you are sure that it will be fitted in the right place first go. I did this and found it to be slightly too close to the edge—that is, the catch was too loose and didn't close the lid tightly. I stuck a piece of card along the bottom edge of the piece and that took up the slack.

23. Mark a line along the inside front edge of the lid that amount from its bottom edge, hold the plate centrally and mark through it the exact positions of the holes and drill. (If you have to place anything dead center that does itself not have a central feature of some sort there is no point in marking a center where it is supposed to go. In this case, measure the full interior length of the lid, subtract the length of the plate from it and divide that by two. Make a mark this distance from one end of the inside of the lid and that is where one end of the plate goes.)

24. Make these holes with the drill bit held in your pin chuck or similar twisted by hand. Be careful not to drill too deep and break through the front—mark the bit with masking tape for safety. Choose the hole size very carefully so that the pins are tight but don't split the wood—test on scrap first.

JOHN BURKE
Watford, Herts, England

(Left and bottom) Box with pin
Oak, mahogany, ebony.
2" x 3¾" x 2¾"

CHARLES B. COBB
Santa Rosa, California
Photos by George Post

Two Boxes from "Wave Top" series
Front: Figured sepale, African bubinga.
6" x 6" x 12"
Back: Maple, Indian bark paper.
12" x 12" x 6"

"Teapot No. 9"
Walnut, African zebra-
wood, Hawaiian Koa,
maple, maple balls painted
copper. Lacquer finish.
Box with removable tray
and storage area
3½" x 3½" x 6"

Three boxes from "Egg" series
Shell formed with cold laminate veneers,
lined with cloth that acts as hinge, walnut
sides and bottom. Carved padauk handle
on left, ebony and brass rod handles on
front and right. Lacquer finish.
6" x 2½" x 3" each

ANDREW CRAWFORD
London, England

"Lapis 4000"
Exterior "double" veneered, first with Macassar ebony then with waney-edged burr yew. Originally intended for storing sample of lapis, the interior of this collector's box features two trays and, hidden behind the hinged front section, three shallow drawers. "Ironwork" strapping and "nails" are all in ebony.
18" x 10½" X 9"

Wall-mounting case for artist's pigments
Exterior veneered with book-matched walnut crotch with detailing in various dyed and natural veneers, mother-of-pearl, and abalone. French polished.
17½" x 26½" X 3", opening as a triptych to 37" wide

Large Watercolor Box
Exterior veneered with book-matched burr sycamore with detailing in box-wood, walnut, dyed veneers, and mother-of-pearl. Features a comprehensively fitted interior including two trays and two drawers in maple.
French polished.
17" x 13" X 5½"

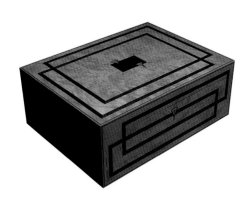

MICHAEL ELKAN
Silverton, Oregon

Two sculptural boxes, with doors,
drawers, and inner boxes

TERRY EVANS
Spiritwood
Olathe, Kansas

Jewelry box
Bird's-eye maple, ebony, cabbage
angelintree.
3" x 10" x 7"

"Burl Arc" lidded container
Spalted maple, maple burl,
dyed black walnut.
17½" x 6¼" x 3⅓"

"Into the Mystic" lidded container
Lacewood, wenge, bird's-eye maple burl.
16⅕" x 7½" x 3⅓"

ROGER & JENNY GIFKINS
Kemsey, England

Oriental box
New Guinea ebony, red
silky oak.
14" x 5⅛" x 4¼"

Jewelry box
Black bean. Marquetry panel by Michael Retter.
13" x 9" x 2¾"

RAY JONES
Asheville, North Carolina
Photos by Tim Barnwell

"Art" boxes with
Spanish cedar drawers
on dovetail slides
Madrone burl, claro
walnut, Indian
tamarind.
8½" x 7¼" x 12½"

Quilted maple,
madrone burl, ebony.
5½" x 7" x 10"

"Hatchbox" series box with four-compartment inner tray
on lazy susan bearing
5½" x 11½" diameter

PO SHUN LEONG
Winnetka, California

Tall box with sliding drawers
Mostly mahogany. 84" high

"Art Boxes" in the form of furniture, inspired by legendary places such as Incan ruins, Mexican and Egyptian pyramids, Chinese temples or American Indian cave dwellings

PETER LLOYD

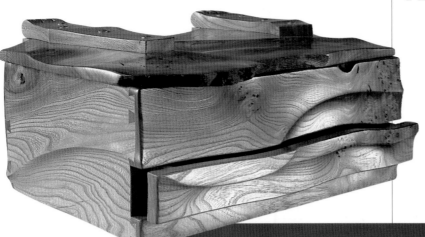

Art boxes with wood
hinges, drawers, and
inner trays

BILL MCDOWELL
Syracuse, New York

(Top and left) Cigar humidor
Curly maple, quarter-sawn wenge.
5" x 8½" x 10½"

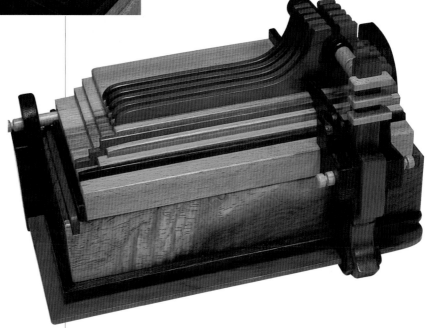

Jewelry box
Cocobolo sapwood, beech,
purple heart and quarter-
sawn wenge.
4½" x 5" x 10"

FIONA MCVEY
Steel Heath Nr Whitchurch
Shropshire, England

Lidded box with dovetailed sides
and inner trays

J. ROBERT SAXBY
Sheffield, South Yorkshire, England

Box with lift-off lid
Routered and carved muninga.

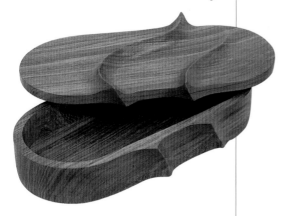

Mantel clock
Laminated yew and rosewood.

Mantel clock of bubinga,
with yew, zebrano, sycamore,
bog oak.

JEFFREY SEATON
Ojai, California

Sculptural "Warrior" box
Walnut, cocobolo, ebony, holly,
copper, and silver tubes.
7" x 7" x 24"

"Abstract" Repousse series
Bird's-eye maple, ebony, holly, black
palm, with red Italian veneer.
6" x 7" x 8"

ERVIN V. SOMOGYI
Berkeley, Califronia

Box designs inspired by the tradition and aesthetic of musical instrument building

Book-matched, edge-joined, musical grade tone woods with mosaic inlay patterns from guitar- and lute-making rosettes.

T. BREEZE VERDANT
Williamsville, Vermont

Lidded box with dovetailed sides and inner tray, all with detailed floral and scenic marquetry

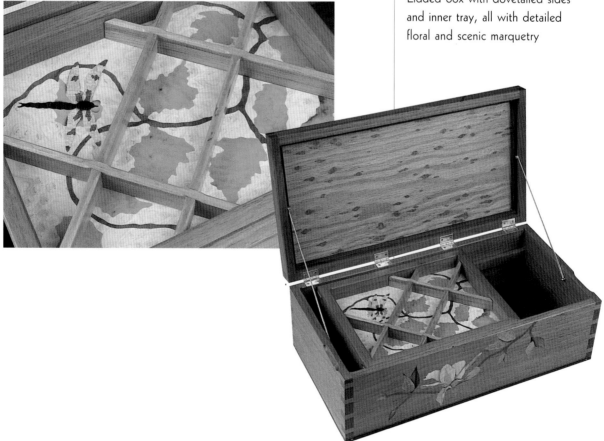

CHRISTOPHER VICKERS
Frome, Somerset, England

Chest with veneered panels, mortise-and-tenon joinery
Bog oak, oak, burr yew.
10" x 10" x 18"

Jewelry box, with removable lined and partitioned inner tray
Tiger oak inset with enamel and copper.
4" x 10" x 14"

English dovetailed chest with butterfly joints, carved plinth, and hand-wrought hinges
Oak.
20" x 24" x 48"

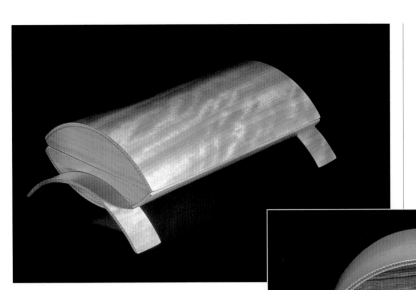

EUGENE F. WATSON
Evergreen, Colorado

Clamshell box
Osage and cocobolo sides, curly
maple top.

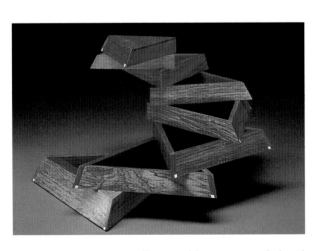

Trapezoid box, open and closed
Bubinga, padauk, and maple inlays.

GREGORY K. WILLIAMS

Burkesville, Kentucky
Photos by Jerry Anthony
Columbus, Ohio

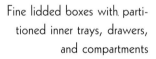

Fine lidded boxes with partitioned inner trays, drawers, and compartments

METRIC versus IMPERIAL

When working in small dimensions there is really no better way than to use the metric system. The imperial system is perfectly good for standard scale joinery and many other jobs. I have provided all of the designs in this book with imperial measurements, because that is what the reader will most likely be most familiar with.

What I suggest is this: Anyone who is happy using imperial measurements, and is used to the mental processes involved in manipulating measurements using $\frac{1}{32}$s and $\frac{1}{64}$s, go right on ahead with my blessing! But for anyone new to small scale work, metric is the way to go!

In my experience of working with the relatively small measurements involved in box-making, using metric has always seemed the obvious way. It's the "slightly more" or "slightly less" that causes problems for me. When you start getting down to $\frac{1}{32}$" it becomes a real mental arithmetical nightmare! For instance, if you want to cut a dimension slightly oversize, what is slightly more than $4\frac{17}{32}$"—even assuming, that is, you can measure that accurately on a feet and inches ruler? I would far rather work out what is slightly more than 112mm (= 113mm—easy!).

One problem with using the imperial system is that for small scale work you will often be using the excessively crowded, subdivided end of a 6" or 12" rule. On this area of an imperial ruler you will often have several different lengths of calibration lines—those for $\frac{1}{4}$", $\frac{1}{8}$", $\frac{1}{16}$" and so on getting progressively shorter and more bunched up, making any genuine attempt to actually measure anything accurately almost impossible. I find that using a ruler simply marked in millimeters down its whole length enables me to measure and mark easily to the nearest $\frac{1}{2}$mm, and even to smaller fractions of a millimeter, assuming halfway decent eyesight and a sharp pencil. This gives an accuracy of down to $\frac{1}{64}$" while being far easier to read and work out.

mm = millimeter
cm = centimeter
m = meter

Foot and Inch Conversions

1 inch = 25.4 mm
1 foot = 304.8 mm

Metric Conversions

1 mm = 0.039 inch
1 m = 3.28 feet

inches	mm	cm	inches	cm	inches	cm
$\frac{1}{8}$	3	0.3	9	22.9	30	76.2
$\frac{1}{4}$	6	0.6	10	25.4	31	78.7
$\frac{3}{8}$	10	1.0	11	27.9	32	81.3
$\frac{1}{2}$	13	1.3	12	30.5	33	83.8
$\frac{5}{8}$	16	1.6	13	33.0	34	86.4
$\frac{3}{4}$	19	1.9	14	35.6	35	88.9
$\frac{7}{8}$	22	2.2	15	38.1	36	91.4
1	25	2.5	16	40.6	37	94.0
$1\frac{1}{4}$	32	3.2	17	43.2	38	96.6
$1\frac{1}{2}$	38	3.8	18	45.7	39	99.1
$1\frac{3}{4}$	44	4.4	19	48.3	40	101.6
2	51	5.1	20	50.8	41	104.1
$2\frac{1}{2}$	64	6.4	21	53.3	42	106.7
3	76	7.6	22	55.9	43	109.2
$3\frac{1}{2}$	89	8.9	23	58.4	44	111.8
4	102	10.2	24	61.0	45	114.3
$4\frac{1}{2}$	114	11.4	25	63.5	46	116.8
5	127	12.7	26	66.0	47	119.4
6	152	15.2	27	68.6	48	121.9
7	178	17.8	28	71.1	49	124.5
8	203	20.3	29	73.7	50	127.0

INDEX